For Simon
many th
L

The mar
beautiful and much
admired.

BLESSED ROGER CADWALLADOR

Cover Image: Stained glass window in St Ethelbert's Church, Leominster, depicting the martyrdom of Blessed Roger Cadwallador.

BLESSED ROGER CADWALLADOR

'GREENWAYS'

THE SEARCH FOR THE MARCHES' HIDDEN SAINT

LYNNE SURTEES

GRACEWING

First published in 2015

Gracewing
2 Southern Avenue
Leominster
Herefordshire HR6 0QF

ISBN 978 0 85244 867 0

Typeset by Action Publishing Technology Ltd
Gloucester GL1 5SR

CONTENTS

This book is for the Catholic People of the Marches
to whom Roger Cadwallador belongs

INTRODUCTION

Introductions are a necessary part of life because, in a curious way, until someone is introduced into a group, he only half exists. Perhaps it was a sense of this shadowy half-existence that prompted Abbot Paul Stonham of Belmont, as chairman of the newly-formed Hereford Catholic History Society, to include Blessed Roger Cadwallador amongst others as being a possible subject for study, and he described the martyr as 'Herefordshire's hidden saint'. I found the Abbot's suggestion intriguing and challenging, and different from anything I had done before. Studying the life of this man, which was so unlike my own, was to prove a fascinating and absorbing adventure.

A friend in the parish provided me with articles from Catholic journals and I bought a *Challoner's Memoirs* and searched the internet. In these, the history of Roger Cadwallador appeared to start and end with his cruel execution, and the articles had titles like 'The Bloody Martyr'. I was sickened and I would have laid my ever-growing stack of articles aside and given up, but the Abbey archivist lent me some papers from the Belmont files, including letters written by Roger Cadwallador, which turned my thinking on its head. Some of the monks of Belmont, starting a hundred years ago, had already laid a foundation of research and translation on which to build. Encouraged and supported throughout by family and friends, not all of them Catholics, I began again. I owe all these people a huge debt of gratitude and cannot thank them enough.

I wanted to be objective in my search, and my working title for this book has always been 'Greenways' as an antidote to 'The Bloody Martyr', first because it was a name he chose for himself and secondly because he was a man of Herefordshire and the

Marches where there are many green ways. I began my search in his birthplace along one of these green ways in Herefordshire at Stretton Sugwas and ended it in Leominster where he was martyred. On the scaffold he declared his love for his own native land and respect for the state but never at the expense of the truths of the Catholic faith and the needs of his endangered flock.

My search revealed that it was the distress of the Roman Catholic faithful at home which brought Roger Cadwallador back from abroad. They were, in Our Lord's words, like sheep without a shepherd. This is not a cosy image, because sheep without a shepherd are in mortal danger. I looked in many books and at pictures and buildings for a sense of those times, including the plays of Shakespeare who was writing contemporaneously. *Hamlet* is thought to have been first performed in 1602 but it may have been as early as 1598, a significant time in the life of Blessed Roger. The play has religious controversy infused throughout. The spirit of Hamlet's father on the battlements of Elsinore cries out in a reproach that is both inconvenient and impossible to ignore:

> Cut off even in the blossoms of my sin,
> Unhous'led, disappointed, unanel'd,
> No reck'ning made, but sent to my account
> With all my imperfections on my head.
> O, horrible! O, horrible! Most horrible! (1.5.76–80)

The archaisms 'unhous'led', 'disappointed', and 'unanel'd' refer to the sacraments of Communion, Penance and Extreme Unction. By his cold-blooded murder, Hamlet's father had been denied the justice of being allowed to die in his religion. The play is a fiction but Shakespeare had put his finger on the dilemma of the Catholic faithful in England which was very real. In depriving them of their priests the Protestant hierarchy had snatched away the Catholic sacraments. Roger Cadwallador was one of that small procession of brave and honourable Roman Catholic priests who, after the Reformation, risked everything to bring the sacramental life back to equally courageous men and women.

Pope Francis exhorts us not to forget our history, in *Evangelii Gaudium* he describes this dimension of our faith as 'deuteronomic' and encourages us to grateful remembrance. The 'believer' is defined by Pope Francis as 'essentially one who remembers'.

Blessed Roger Cadwallador was plucked from obscurity by Saint John Paul II. He was among the 1,340 men and women he beatified in an act of solidarity for the gift of their lives which they had given to the Church over the centuries – lest we forget. It was an especially poignant action by a remarkable man who was the first-ever Polish pope. He spent the first fifty-eight years of his life in Poland and would never forget the Warsaw Rising and the Holocaust. By hiding in a basement he narrowly escaped capture on 6 August 1944, 'Black Sunday', when 8,000 young Polish men in Krakow had been rounded up and never returned. He endured nearly half a century of Communism, during which time the persecuted Church was an ever-present reality, and these years coloured all his decisions and public pronouncements. Today the same forces are brought to bear on the Church as the horror and terror inflicted on the faithful has not gone away and the Church continues to be persecuted and the noble army of martyrs continues to grow.

Roger Cadwallador is the calm centre of my book. I cannot describe him to you in intimate detail because I do not know whether or not he smoked a pipe or what colour his eyes were. I have searched as far as I can for his place in the context of the time in which he lived and proved to my own satisfaction that this was a man who was incredibly brave and unimpeachably holy. He lived and died for his Saviour and for the priesthood and for the Catholic people of his own beloved country, England. The story of Blessed Roger Cadwallador might be considered by some to be a tragedy but it certainly would not have been thought so by him. He died trusting in eternal justice and in the deeper reality which promised that the scaffold on which he suffered and was martyred was the gateway to everlasting happiness.

Lynne Surtees
27 August 2014

CHAPTER 1

The Roman Road

THE ROMAN ROAD, which ran from 'Cena's' Roman fort at Kenchester Magnis to Stretton Grandison, gave its name to the medieval village of Stretton. The Old English 'straet' means street, and the village straddled the road. Stretton was the birthplace of Roger Cadwallador. The Roman road still exists as the A4103. Take the A4103 from Hereford towards Wales and pass the sign for Stretton Sugwas. On the right-hand side of the road there is a sign for 'The Priory'. Follow the track to 'The Priory'. Stretton Court is on the left and the remains of the graveyard of the original Stretton church are on the right.

The Stretton[1] Roger Cadwallador would have known is now one of Herefordshire's two hundred or so deserted, ruined medieval villages. Over a stream there is still a little medieval bridge that carries the road to Credenhill. Between the bridge and Stretton Court Farm, which is beside Stretton Court, is the site of the deserted village. Today only the earthworks remain in a very stony field. Nearby are two ponds with traces of two ground water-works. Although the present Sutton Court is Georgian, one of the over-mantels inside is dated 1598. Roger is known to have celebrated Mass at Stretton Court at the time.

Along the lane from Stretton Court is the Priory Hotel which was once Stretton vicarage. The foundations of the old church are in the grounds of Stretton Court, and in front and to the left of the hotel are the remains of the old churchyard which still contains gravestones. The new parish church of St Mary Magdalene,[2] across the road in Stretton Sugwas, incorporates some features of the old

Norman church and it is likely that Roger would have known these.

The Victorian architect, Cheiake, reused timbers from the original church for the black and white tower as well as the medieval windows and three Norman doorways. Above one of these doorways, inside the church, there is a tympanum of Sampson and the lion. The carving of the tympanum is credited to two local schools of international renown: the carvers of Brinksop for the major part of the work, but credit is given to the Kilpeck carvers for the lion's Viking head. They would simply have delighted the heart and mind of a small boy of Tudor times.

The font is attributed to another school of local carvers from Castle Frome and it dates from the middle of the fourteenth century. If, as has been suggested, Roger Cadwallador was a convert he may well have been baptised in this font. Also, in the vestry there are some fifteenth-century heraldic tiles from the old church on which he may have walked.

Roger would have known another work of art in the new church, a slab monument to Richard Grevelhey and his wife who died in 1473. The slab is beautifully worked; there is an incised black line portrait of the couple, she with a butterfly head-piece, and he in a fur-trimmed gown. This elegant couple were inhabitants of Stretton less than a hundred years before Roger's birth. They too lived in interesting times from the beginning of the Age of Discovery on the world stage, to the more local Wars of the Roses which brought the Tudors to the throne for more than one hundred years.

Roger Cadwallador was born sometime between 1556 and 1568, the eldest son of a yeoman, also called Roger, and his wife Margaret. It would appear that Roger Senior, between 1600 and 1603, at a point soon after the return of his priest son to the English Mission, moved to Treville, leaving his lands in Stretton to the care of his younger son and heir, John. At the end of the sixteenth century, there is a record of a summons to a church court in the Weobley Deanery under the Stretton heading, written in

Latin, that, when translated reads: 'Cadwallador, Roger did not receive the Eucharist and does not frequent church.'[3] It may have been that the Cadwallador family was being watched, and the move to Treville may suggest a desire to provide a sanctuary for his son, Roger, when he returned, and to distance himself from his main property in Stretton which was being managed by John.

In his will, made in 1603, Roger Senior states that he is 'of Treville', a parish without a church. Treville occupied part of the area which lay at the heart of the Martyr's spiritual care. Treville Wood is recorded in the Domesday Book. The great oaks which formed it had been felled in Elizabeth's reign and it was designated afterwards as Treville Park, although there is evidence that the oaks were being replaced by Sir Charles Morgan. It covered a large area stretching from Kingstone and Thruxton in the north to Abbeydore in the west, and to the south and east by Saint Devereux, and was part of the Golden Valley.

Treville was a source of irritation to those collecting tithes for King James I, who tried to claim that he owned the rectory or church of the Park of Treville, never mind that the buildings did not appear to have existed. Sir Charles Morgan was the chief landowner in Treville Park and lived in the Hall, although there were probably about fifteen or so other gentry who owned or leased part of the 2,000 or more acres of the Park.[4]

Treville was cleverly managed and it would have taken considerable acumen to prosper despite the strong links with recusancy, and it occurs more than once in the search for Roger Cadwallador. An entry in the church courts record for Stretton, 1603–4, which is a record of his father's death and burial in Stretton where there was a churchyard, indicates that this was the case. It refers to

Cadwallador, Roger defunt – Thomas Vaughan warned before Jacob Baillie [perhaps the magistrate] answered that William Morgan of the Parke (Treville) was present at the said burial, William Browne of Madley, Richard Howell Phillips of Eaton Bishop and John and Jacob Cadwallador and John Griffiths of

Kingstone for what is described in the margin of the court record as a 'burial at night' without minister.[5]

The priest-son of the deceased may have been present, as the date suggests that he was back in Herefordshire at that time. If so, Thomas Vaughan turned a blind eye. Four of those named were reported to be at the 'Commotion at Allensmore' in 1605, which will be discussed later. They were not let off with just a warning after 'the Commotion', as they were at this illegal burial, which shows how the screw had tightened on recusants in the short space of two years and how increasingly important the loyal faithful thought it was to protect their priest, as at Allensmore they came in numbers, and armed.

The will of the Martyr's father mentions William Morgan, the son of Sir Charles Morgan, clearly a family friend, who appears at significant times in Roger's life. The following is part of his father's will, which helps to place Roger in the context of his family. It was drawn up in 1603, the year of the accession of James I, and was proved in 1610, the year of Blessed Roger's martyrdom.[6] The will reads:

> In the name of God Amen. I Roger Cadwallader of Treville doe make my last will and testament in manner and forme following, firste I commend my soul to god my maker and Jesus Christe my redeemer and my body to be buried in Christian burial
>
> Item whereas my brother Morris is to paye me twenty shillings a yeare for divers years yet to come and two shillings a yeare for ever the said twenty shillings a yeare I give and bequeath to the poore people of Stretton where my executors shall think good and the two shillings of perpetual Rente I give to maintaine the service of god there as my executors shall thincke goode
>
> Item all my lands in Stretton I give to Johnne my sonne and his heires for ever and my goodes and cattells to Margaret my wife and John my sonne.

The next item relates to debt to be paid and debt to be recalled:

> when the parties are able to pay. Lastly I do ordaine and appointe
> Margaret my wife and John my son executors of this my last will
> and testament and my deare freend maister William Morgan the
> overseer.

The duty of care for his eldest son, which the maker of the will was
passing to his family and his son's closest friend in choosing them
as executors and overseer, is perhaps implicit in the provision of
the final, well-funded resting place.

The level of risk for those closest to a priest was very high and
their faith and courage would be tested. In December 1605, John
Cadwallador was summoned before the Stretton church court as
an executor for the will of 'Roger Kadd'lr' (Cadwallador) and the
church wardens presented 'viva voce' the accusation that he had
suppressed a sum with regard to his father's will. He was
summoned to the next court and excommunicated to the 'gravest
level'.[7]

Roger, the subject of my search, lived for the great majority of
his life, during the long reign of Elizabeth Tudor. His background
was 'respectable' rather than aristocratic. In a reference to his father
in 1600, it is recorded that Roger Cadwallador of Stretton was
assessed in a lay levy for tax £3. Four other people were assessed
with him: one (a gentleman) at £3, one other at £3, and two more
at 20s, which would indicate that he was among the county gentry.
It was sometime between 1600, the date of the lay tax, and 1603,
when he made his will, that he moved to Treville.

He was said to have an income of thirty pounds a year, which
means that he would have been rich enough to own his own house
and employ servants, but he and his family may well have worked
with them. There is later evidence from documents kept in the
County records that these lands were extensive, including
Westfield where there is a Garden Centre today. A document from
1671, included in the Register of Papist Estates of 1717–1753,

mentions lands leased in these areas by yet another Roger Cadwallador. In 1705 Jane Cadwallador of Stretton, described as a spinster, which may mean that she was a child at the time, with John Phillips her guardian, was recorded to be leasing land again in Westfield.

Roger, as the son of a 'gentleman farmer', would have learnt to plough and to sow and to help with the harvest. Major crops,[8] demanding the most attention, were sheep and forestry. Sheep were tended by Tudor farmers for their fleeces as well as their milk. Sheep's milk was used to make cheese as well as for nurturing babies up to four years old. It would have been death to drink water and so, from childhood, everyone drank ale made from barley grown on the farm. Sheep also provided more sheep by lambing twice a year and then, when they were past being useful in other ways, they provided meat in the form of mutton. The young Roger would have learnt shepherding skills as a boy and climbed the local hills to bring the flock down from higher to lower pastures for winter grazing.

As he grew older, Roger would have become expert at managing the woods on his father's land. Trees were an important commodity as everything from timber-framed houses and ships to furniture and fences were made of wood. The woodlands also yielded foraged foods, including nuts and acorns, and medicines derived from hips and haws. The ubiquitous pig rooted on the forest floor, growing fat on a harvest of acorns so that eventually it would feed a family for months. The scaffold which was made for Blessed Roger's martyrdom may well have been built from timber grown in local woods.

Roger Cadwallador would have had an intimate knowledge of the land, which would have stood him in good stead during the years when he was hunted. Then he, priest and scholar as he was, would have been able to turn his hand to practically anything.

Notes

1   M. Raven, *A Guide to Herefordshire* (Hereford: Michael Raven, 1996), pp. 187–188.

2   N. Pevsner, *The Buildings of England, Herefordshire* (London: Penguin, 1990), pp. 295–296.

3   Entry for Weobley Deanery under Stretton, Hereford Archives, HRO HD4/1/157, 1598–9.

4   Hereford Archives, TNA E134/8Jas1)/Hil9, 1611.

5   Entry in church courts for Stretton, Hereford Archives, HRO HD4/1/161, 1603–4.

6   National Archives, *Transcription of the will of Roger Cadwallador of Trevill*, 1603, PRO 11/115/134.

7   Church court records Stretton, Hereford Archives, HRO4/1/162.

8   H.P.R. Finberg, *The Agrarian History of England and Wales, Volume 4, 1500–1640* (Cambridge: Cambridge University Press, 1967), pp. 104–106.

CHAPTER 2

'Scolis Gramaticis Angliae'

A MONG THE PRIVATE PAPERS kept at Belmont Abbey is a note[1] which reports that from his earliest days Roger Cadwallador was unworldly. Another contemporary record[2] states that even as a boy he was 'assiduous in serving God, and learning his books, wherein he surpassed most of his school-fellows'. 'School-fellows' is evidence that he went to school. This document calls him Rogers, the alias he used frequently as a missionary priest in those perilous times.

A little later in his career another source[3] records that Roger Greenways, the first recorded use of this alias, was 'educatus in litteris humanioribus en Scolis Gramaticis Angliae'. This suggests that he went to an English Grammar School and was not educated privately at home by a resident schoolmaster or priest, as the sons of the gentry often were.

The senior Roger Cadwallador, the father of Roger and his younger brother John, may have been a Church Papist,[4] one who attended Church of England services as required by the state, but secretly considered himself to be a Catholic. A definition of 1582 described such people as 'Papists which can keep their consciences in private'. Others intended to be reconciled to the Catholic Church on their deathbed. Not a few male Church Papists were the heads of households who had an arrangement with their wives whereby the wives would continue in the Old Faith in private and might raise their children in it, with the exception of the eldest son. It is clear from his father's will that Roger Cadwallador the Younger had renounced his right to be his father's heir, although accounts and letters show that he continued to have the love and support of his family.

Women at that time had no rights in common law and this lack of rights and property and the ostensible Anglicanism of their menfolk meant that it was extremely difficult to impose a fine upon a recusant woman. 'Anglican' is used regularly throughout this text for convenience as one of the names for members of the 'Church of England' although neither name was in use during Roger's lifetime.

This did not mean that any of these Papist men and women wished that the King of Spain had sailed triumphantly up the Thames at the time of the Armada to be crowned King of England in Westminster Abbey. Or that Mary Queen of Scots, because she probably connived at the murder of her husband and constantly plotted for the English crown, should replace their Elizabeth of whom they were not yet tired.

'The falling away from Catholic unity is an event so strange and so terrible as to require some further explanation' reflects the *Catholic Encyclopedia* in its section on Henry VIII. This suggests that the 'brutal passion and selfish policy' of that tyrant was only a secondary cause and sees the problem as stemming from 'direct hostility to Papal domination'. This does not appear to have been Roger Cadwallador's opinion or the opinion of others who remained faithful Papists in the face of extraordinary persecution.

The Council of Trent,[5] recognising the problems of the Reformation, had begun its long series of meetings which were to continue from 1534 to 1549. Although it is acknowledged to have been Spirit-led, outward-looking and with a humanist ethos, and regarded as being at the heart of the Counter-Reformation, it had hardly begun to penetrate into England. It was a work of love for priests like Roger to introduce to the country new approaches enshrined in the Counter-Reformation.

By the grace of conviction and perseverance, the Catholics of Herefordshire clung to their religion. The Marches were a notably conservative area, far away from the glitter and clamour of Elizabeth's court. Like many others, Roger's father may have been devoted to Queen and country as well as the Old Faith. Sophistry was a cloak for their consciences that all Catholics appear to have been required to wear.

There is evidence that Roger Senior may have been the sower of the seed of his eldest son's vocation. In a letter from prison, Roger records that there was a crisis in his childhood, perhaps a terrible accident or life-threatening illness. He refers the reader to his mother and this letter may explain his conversion to Catholicism and the strong influence of his father:

> Remember I pray you my humble dutie to my mother. She can tell (for I have often heard my father speake of yt) that when I was in my childhood dangerously sicke, he made a vow or prmse to God that if I recovered, he would bestow me on him.

Roger, in common with other children of those times, would have started his schooling at a 'Petty' or 'Dame' School, conducted in the house of a teacher. These schools were run by a local, well-educated housewife or an old man and provided education for middle-class boys between the ages of five and seven. The curriculum had become standardised and even in 'Petty' schools the schoolmaster or -mistress was tested by a sort of Tudor Ofsted for soundness of religion. Reading and writing were secondary to the acquisition of virtue and piety. As a minimum requirement every child was expected to learn by heart, and be able to recite, the Ten Commandments, the twelve articles of the Apostles' Creed, and the Lord's Prayer. A child would only be able to proceed to grammar school when he was able to read for himself from the wealth that Holy Scripture contained. The Lord's Prayer and the words when making the Sign of the Cross, 'In the name of the Father...,' which were used as an exorcism to drive the devil from young scholars, were written on a wooden paddle covered in translucent horn which was the vehicle for learning the alphabet, vowels and syllables. The more advanced ABC was often combined with a simplified catechism. A thorough knowledge of

Latin, even as early as six years of age, was a sign of a superior
education. From the start a child would have been grounded in
English or English-Latin grammar. In addition, the boy Roger
would have learnt arithmetic, or what was called 'casting of
accounts', in Petty school.

Education, for the young Roger, between the ages of seven and
fourteen, may have continued at Hereford School,[6] the local
grammar school (*scolis gramaticis*), the site of which was probably
in the cloisters of the Cathedral. In the reign of Edward VI, the
western side of the Bishop's cloister was burnt down and on this
site a School Room[7] was built. There is no record of what it was
built of or its size, but it probably had an entrance from what we
know as Palace Yard with windows overlooking the Lady Arbour. If
Roger attended the school, it was at a time 'when good work was
carried on in it':

> Hereford was then in the eyes of the world a very much more
> important city than now; it was indeed looked upon as the centre
> for South Wales. The Courts of the Council of the Marches and
> Wales, and subsequently the Assizes for a huge district, were
> frequently held here, prisoners being brought for trial from South
> Wales. It was then considered quite as important a town as Cardiff
> is now; indeed the laws of the latter, like many other places, were
> copied from ours. It was not therefore so extraordinary for the
> Dean and Chapter to request that a School for South Wales should
> be established here.[8]

The weekly timetable of a Tudor schoolboy such as Roger was
demanding. Boys would have attended six days a week. In the
winter the school day started at seven o'clock. This was in order to
save on the cost of candles which the boys provided themselves. In
the summertime, school started an hour earlier and ended as dusk
fell at about five o'clock. There would have been a fifteen-minute
break for breakfast in the morning and an hour at lunchtime.

On Monday there would be an examination which was based on
the Sunday sermon. On Tuesday to Thursday the basic curriculum

included repetition and constant testing of languages (mainly Latin until the age of ten when a boy would begin to learn Greek), as well as lessons in grammar, theology, history, rhetoric, logic, philosophy, arithmetic, literature, geometry and religious studies. On Friday there would be Examinations and Punishments. The punishment, usually birching, would have been administered by the school master. It was very much the accepted rule that to spare the rod was to spoil the child. On Saturday the boys would study the catechism and arithmetic.

Great stress was put on learning the Bible throughout, especially the Old Testament, and the emphasis was on *Ecclesiasticus* and *Proverbs*.[9] *Ecclesiasticus* was read in English from the age of seven; it was translated into Latin and back into the vernacular by the age of ten. This would have perfected the child's knowledge of his own native language as well as Latin. *Ecclesiasticus* was read aloud along with other books of the Bible every day at dinner and supper. This book and *Proverbs* were considered to be an effective way of conveying the wisdom of a father to his offspring. The received wisdom was that the world was a dangerous place.

Ecclesiasticus Chapter 2, starts with some very prescient and poignant words in the light of what was to follow:

> My son if you aspire to serve the Lord, prepare yourself for an ordeal. Be sincere of heart, be steadfast, and do not be alarmed when disaster comes. Cling to him and do not leave him, so that you may be honoured at the end of your days. Whatever happens to you, accept it, and the uncertainties of your humble state, since gold is tested in the fire, and chosen men, in the furnace of humiliation. Trust him and he will uphold you, follow a straight path and hope in him. You, who fear the Lord, wait for his mercy; do not turn aside in case you fall. You, who fear the Lord, trust him and you will not be baulked of your reward. (Eccl 2:1–8)

The boys who emerged from the grammar schools could not have been untouched by these influences. *Ecclesiasticus* and *Proverbs*, with their deeply moral theology, which occasionally seems to edge towards paranoia, are said by scholars to have profoundly influenced Shakespeare. Search *Hamlet* and *King Lear* to find evidence of this, and Roger Cadwallador was no less a child of those suspicious and litigious times than Shakespeare.

It would appear that Roger left Hereford Grammar School a well-educated youth, disciplined and self-controlled. By the standards of the day he had been taught to be scholarly but not pedantic, well informed, and able to present a reasoned argument with good humour and wit. More than just a good scholar, he is said to have had a rare 'genius' for learning. Above all this, in the real sense of the word, he was God-fearing. At the age of fourteen, the education of boys would continue at university, usually Oxford or Cambridge, where they would be in residence for seven years.

It is a matter of record that these two universities began to be purged of Roman Catholics during the 1560s. This is because Catholics felt unable to take the Oath of Supremacy which was a necessity for membership of the universities. The oath recognised Elizabeth as the Supreme Governor of the Church of England, and to swear it would have denied papal jurisdiction. There is no record of Roger Cadwallador attending either of these establishments although he was a considerable scholar. It would seem that he went abroad.

The search continues in France.

Notes

1   Belmont Papers, Note from volume 2 of the *Catholic Record.*
2   Belmont Papers, Fragment from *Douai Manuscript.*
3   Belmont Papers, quoting from *The Valladolid Diaries, 1593.*
4   A. Frazer, *The Gunpowder Plot* (St Ives: Orion Books, 2002), pp. 31–32.
5   'Counter-Reformation', (Encyclopaedia Britannica Online, latest edition).
6   W.T. Carless, *A Short History of Hereford School* (Hereford: Wilson and Phillips, 1914), p. 14.
7   *Ibid.*, p. 18.
8   *Ibid.*, p. 16.
9   L.B. Smith, *Treason in Tudor England* (Princeton, NJ: Princeton University Press, 1986), pp. 72–117.

CHAPTER 3

A Priest Ordained Abroad

His desire of improving himself in religion and study carried him beyond the seas, where he entered himself a student in Douay College at that time residing at Rheims. Of this college he was an alumnus, and having made great progress in learning and virtue, he received there most of his orders.[1]

NOTHING WOULD HAVE PREPARED Roger Cadwallador for Rheims. The ancient city with its soaring, beautiful cathedral was a testimony to the riches of the Catholic Faith of which he believed himself to be an heir. At every altar in every wonderful church the sacrifice of the Mass would be offered in the same language that he would have used in the Schools and for reading and writing. The music that accompanied the Mass was newly composed to make the words of the liturgy as understandable and meaningful as possible, a pattern for sacred church music to the present day.

Rheims was a royal city with many splendid buildings where kings of France had been crowned and entertained for a thousand years. Here cathedrals, churches and abbeys were cherished, not sold or stripped or sacked. Here Christ's holy mother Mary was treated with the reverence she deserves. Here shrines and relics were treated with due respect. Undisturbed in the abbey was housed the Holy Ampulla, containing the Sacred Chrism brought by the Holy Spirit in the form of a dove to St Remy, for whom the city was named. It was used for the anointing of King Clovis before his coronation and in the coronation ceremonial for succeeding kings of France. It was not considered a superstition to treat it reverently. A sacred, royal and scholarly city, it appears to have been Blessed Roger's home for the next ten years.

Before its temporary transfer to Rheims in 1568, the English College at Douai[2] was in Spanish Flanders. The already considerable numbers of English Catholics in residence before 1559 had made their influence felt, and many of the traditions of Catholic Oxford were perpetuated at Douai, and many of the chief posts were held by fellows of Oxford colleges in the foundation of the University. There were five faculties: theology, canon law, civil law, medicine, and arts. William, later Cardinal, Allen became Regius Professor of Divinity after taking his licentiate at Douai in 1560.

It is not surprising therefore that when William Allen conceived his idea for a college abroad, having for its purpose the perpetuation of the Catholic Faith of England, he should settle on Douai and gather up some of the many scattered English Catholics, who had been forced to leave England, and give them a base for their studies.

The Belmont papers say that Roger Cadwallador had been taken notice of at Douai by a tutor, Dr Pits, for his rare genius for learning, and great knowledge in the Greek tongue. In addition Latin, familiar since childhood, would have been second-nature to him. It may be that with his prodigious talent for languages, he was involved in continuing the work of the translation from the Latin Vulgate into English. The Council of Trent had recognised the need for a translation of the Bible into the several languages of the principal provinces of the Latin Church. Work on the New Testament had already been completed and published in 1582 but work continued on the Old Testament and the Apocrypha all the time that he was in Rheims, until it too was published in Douai in 1609.

The aim was to produce a Bible totally faithful to the Latin Vulgate, the work of Saint Jerome at the end of the fourth century, because 'there were heretical translations poisoning the people'.[3] It would seem that printing was not then an unmixed blessing any more than the internet is today.

The Douai-Rheims Bible was remarkably faithful to the original Vulgate which is the principal Latin version of the Bible revised in 1592, adopted as the official text for the Roman Catholic Church. 'Vulgate' comes from the Latin *vulgare* meaning 'to make common'. In reality such a direct and truthful translation was to be a problem as a dogmatic translation from Latin into English sometimes made the meaning obscure and rather difficult to convey in public reading.

A Puritan theologian and Master of Pembroke, Cambridge, William Fulke,[4] railed against the Rheims version of the New Testament. He printed the text side by side with that of the *Bishops' Bible*, which was the official English version until the *King James Version* in 1611. Ironically, that led to it becoming widely known in England and opened the way for its influence on the language of the *Authorised Version* of King James I.

One of the major outcomes of the Council of Trent was ecclesiastical and structural change so that the growing divide between clergy and the laity was addressed. Parish priests were to be better educated in matters of theology and apologetics and the faithful were to be helped to understand the nature of art and liturgy. Notebooks and handbooks became more common, describing how to be good priests and confessors. Practices which had brought the Church into disrepute, such as the selling of indulgences to build the Basilica of St Peter, were replaced by a return to earlier Catholic models of humanism and devotion to, and careful observance of, the faith. The Roman Missal, the Catechism and the Tridentine Mass all resulted from the Council of Trent. Legalism, which is a strict adherence to a literal interpretation of the religious laws of the Church, was insisted upon. Discipline was improved and the parish was emphasized. It was ground-breaking training for the priesthood.

The Council of Trent upheld the basic structure of the Medieval Church, its sacramental system, religious orders and doctrine. It rejected all compromise with Protestantism. The Real Presence in the Mass was reaffirmed. Pilgrimages and the veneration of saints and relics were encouraged as commendable practices.

It was in the light of all this that Roger began to be formed into a priest. Allen's confident aim was that when the time came for the re-establishment of Catholicism there should be a body of learned clergy schooled in the Catholic Faith to return to England. Douai was the first college organised according to the rules and constitution of the Council of Trent.

The English College of Douai transferred to Rheims in 1578 and did not return until 1593 by which time Cardinal William Allen had been called to reside in Rome. His dream that England would return to the Catholic Faith in his lifetime had evaporated and by the time Roger Cadwallador was ordained there was martyrdom in the air.

Young seminarians who were full of zeal for the faith and who were prepared to lay down their lives were not being radicalised in the way that terrorist extremists prepare young suicide bombers today. They were missionaries, whose aim was to lift the drooping spirits of the faithful in England and maintain orthodoxy. Just as a subaltern in the Great War was aware before battle that he might be killed and was prepared to sacrifice his life, equally for the young seminarian, martyrdom was an ever-present reality. Reading between the lines it is not difficult to see that considerable thought must have gone into the matter of martyrdom, not least by Roger Cadwallador who at Rheims was said by Dr Pits to have 'a great talent for controversy'. This excellent talent for debate was considered to be very advantageous as it meant that Roger could express himself well in passionate and strongly-worded argument. This quality would hold him in very good stead if he was ever to stand up for the Faith under harsh and unfriendly questioning.

Martyrdom was not to be sought, just the opposite. If it had been sought it would not have been martyrdom but suicide. It was important to take sensible precautions such as disguise, aliases, and hiding to avoid it. It was important to prepare so that one could defend the Catholic Faith without equivocation if examined. To be a martyr it was essential that one died in *odium fides*, that is because of hatred of the Faith and not for treason.

A priest who was tested in this way would have needed a great deal of support. If God chose a man to be one of his blessed martyrs then it was the duty of all brother priests and Catholic laity to assist him in accomplishing this glorious outcome in whatever way they could, and to make it known afterwards, without being involved in the act itself, and to record the event for posterity.

The harsh reality was that by the end of the sixteenth century there were 366 priests working in the English Mission. Fifty of them were survivors of the old Marian Priests who were ordained in England at the time of Mary Tudor, 300 priests were from Douai and the other foreign seminaries, and sixteen from the Society of Jesus. Of these, 128 priests were martyred for their faith.

It is a matter of record that using the alias Rogers, Roger Cadwallador was ordained sub-deacon at Rheims on 21 September 1591, and deacon by Cardinal Sega the following 24 February in 1592. In August 1592, he was sent with three others to Valladolid in Spain, where Cardinal Allen had recently founded a new college, to finish his studies and be ordained a priest. He and his three companions, leaving Rheims after they had been made deacons, may have followed the pilgrim route in France which ends eventually in Santiago de Compostela. It is a reasonable supposition that the 'Way Houses' along the pilgrim way would have provided rest and support for these holy young men. After they crossed the Pyrenees, Spain would have been laid out in front of them. The four men would have left 'the Way' at this point.

It may have been that the establishment at Rheims had the Council of Trent in mind when these young men were sent to Spain. The Council had included figures who added spirituality to the movement. Among them, the Spanish mystics and reformers of the Carmelite order, particularly St Teresa of Avila and St John of the Cross, focussed on the interior conversion to Christ. St John's passion for suffering and to accept it for oneself may have resonated with the young Cadwallador, raised as he was in a tradition that venerates the saints. Although St Teresa died in 1582 and St John of the Cross in 1591, they left their writings, and the new order of Discalced Carmelites, which they had established in Avila, was continuing their work to great effect. Both of these great saints travelled widely in Spain and their influence would have been felt especially throughout the region around Valladolid. Roger and his three companions, may have been sent to learn as much as they could of the 'mystical mind' in order to strengthen and preserve their souls for what lay ahead.

This may have been the plan but it was a marathon excursion for a relatively brief stay in Spain. At this point it is reasonable to consider other possibilities for this long journey which would include an examination of the practice of politics and statesmanship at the time. When Elizabeth Tudor advanced to the crown in 1558 she departed from the 'Old Faith' re-established by Mary Tudor. She was zealous in the propagation of her version of the Church of England which appears to have been based on her father's version of Catholicism without the Pope. Conversely she also resisted the urge to meddle in the consciences of others and for several years there was a peaceable, though private enjoyment of the 'Old Faith'. For a number of reasons this was not to last.

In spite of the worsening situation, diplomatic activities never ceased between England and her Catholic neighbours and it is the nature of diplomacy to compromise. Funded by Spanish money while they were in Valladolid, it may have been that Blessed Roger and others, including another martyr, Blessed Robert Drurie, were to be prepared to restore Catholicism to England in the kinder, gentler light of the Counter-Reformation. This was in opposition to the more conservative Jesuits who considered it a sacred tenet that the Pope had absolute supremacy over the monarch. This was so much so that the more conciliatory approach taken by others was abhorrent to the Jesuits, especially those living out of England in exile. Although it was to change later, at that time they were prepared to 'assist' the Pope by deposing a given monarch and indeed they felt it was their duty – Jesuits were the Pope's sworn men. The disastrous, in the opinion of many, Papal Bull of Pius V in 1570 excommunicating 'the bastard' Elizabeth was grist for their mill, as the Bull gave an assassin the moral right to remove her.

It is clear from the Belmont archives that Roger Cadwallador, a Secular priest, belonged to a different party from those who lived in the peace and security of their enclosures, as well as from the Jesuits who are attached to an Order, the Society of Jesus, and were known as Regulars. Cardinal Allen had to defend his seminary priests who were criticised for being too young, as well as for wearing secular dress and decking themselves out with feathers, presumably in their hats. The Cardinal,[5] replying to a critical letter from Maurice Chauncey, Prior of the English Carthusians, champions his young priests first by reminding the Prior that they are all above the canonical age of twenty-five. Then he lists some of the perils to which they will be exposed, unlike those who take their rest in this life. These include night journeys in terrible weather, the risk of thieves, of spies and false brethren; the need to hide in huge discomfort in holes where they cannot have fires or candles because this would give them away to the enemy. This is not all they will have to suffer. William Allen, who appears to have been a prophet as well as a great prelate, reminds those who complain that, in addition, they will have to rise from their beds at midnight to avoid the searches of those who hate them and if they are caught they will be rewarded with disgrace and worse, and the reason for all this is a desire to win the souls of their dearest coun-trymen. He asks if this is not enough of a penance for their feathers. It was only three months after this letter of 1577 that the first of his young priests was martyred by being hacked to death.

The detractors of some of the Seculars criticised what they saw as a willingness to accept the *status quo* in order to establish Catholicism as an unthreatening, minority religion which would be officially tolerated. This would mean that the 'deposing' power of the Pope was no longer accepted. Blessed Roger's letters give one the impression of a cheerful, hopeful character. His party's aim was to re-establish Catholic orthodoxy in England peacefully, step by step, with the cooperation of their beloved country and while there was still goodwill for the cause they loved.

The Jesuits in Rome appear to have seen this position as lacking integrity because for them the initiative would always come from the Pope, and Elizabeth and the Protestant establishment and even the English people would have nothing to do with it. Leading Jesuits appear to have been blinkered with regard to the heir to Elizabeth I; they believed that it was possible to force a Catholic successor on the country, who would be subject to the Pope. The succession was a constant source of speculation and discussion and this was partly Elizabeth's fault as she saw it as an issue to avoid. However the undermining of the English crown by Roman Catholics abroad was, without doubt, having a harmful effect on Roman Catholics and Catholicism at home.

Roger Cadwallador was to become an Appellant, that is one of those thirty-three Secular priests who put their names to the Appeal to the Pope against the administration of an Archpriest who was overseen by the Jesuits, and to stress that in his place they wanted a Bishop. Their hope was not that Catholicism should be imposed from outside but it should be an officially accepted religion, tolerated by the state. He had been identified in Rheims as having the intellect and conviction which would have been necessary to carry the Seculars' policy forward and this may have been the reason that he had been sent to Spain. Blessed Robert Drurie who, it is thought, was hung, drawn and quartered at Tyburn in 1607, was already a seminarian at Valladolid and was later an 'Appellant'. Roger spoke of being 'yoked' with Robert Drurie when he heard of the martyrdom of his friend shortly before his own death. It is speculation, but it may have been that a cluster of like-minded young priests was being brought together and this may have been an alternative reason for the long diversion to Valladolid.

It was an exciting time to be in Spain as this was the Age of Discovery. Spain and Portugal were enjoying a sixty-year-long period of Unification and artists like El Greco were being drawn to the court of Philip II. That court was shortly to transfer temporarily to Valladolid, formerly an Arabic city famous for its art and architecture. In addition, Spain was colossally wealthy, being fed with riches from the Indies and it was the banker to the Counter-Reformation.

In the archives of Roger Cadwallador held at Belmont, there is a picture taken from a painting kept at the seminary in Valladolid. Looked at with the eye of faith, it is the portrait of a man at the height of his physical, intellectual and spiritual powers. He is slim and strongly built, not surprisingly as walking from Rheims to Valladolid would have made him physically fit. There is elegance in his clothing and in his hands and his features. He is dark-haired and bearded and has large eyes which gaze into the distance, and his expression is intelligent and watchful. He is turning slightly as if to listen to the child angel who holds the martyr's crown above his head. Behind him there is a picture within the picture of two angels greeting the Blessed Martyr preparing to lead him into Paradise.

In the Cadwallador chapel in the church of St Ethelbert in Leominster, there is a stained-glass window commemorating Roger's martyrdom. The portrait of Blessed Roger appears to be taken from the Valladolid picture as the pose is the same. The chapel is on the south side of the church which is said to have been built on the site where one of the martyr's quarters is said to have been displayed.

The record shows that Roger and three companions left Rheims on 21 August 1592. They arrived in Valladolid on 3 January 1593. Roger was using the name Greenways, and was probably aged twenty-seven. It is recorded at the English College that he was ordained to the priesthood in August 1593 by the Bishop of Zamora. Soon after his ordination to the priesthood he was sent to the English Mission. He set off on the long journey for England, and probably arrived home in 1594. He would already have been aware that he was returning to a country of plots, paranoia and persecution. When he set foot on English soil the grisly skulls and mutilated corpses displayed throughout the realm were evidence enough that men and women risked their lives for both good and bad reasons and of the horrible consequences if they failed.

Notes

1   Belmont Papers, from '*The Douay Record*'.
2   F.L. Cross (ed.), *Oxford Dictionary of the Christian Church* (London: Oxford University Press, 1957), pp. 418–419.
3   'Douay Bible', (Catholic Encyclopedia, online).
4   F.L. Cross (ed.), *Oxford Dictionary of the Christian Church*, p. 532.
5   Godfrey Anstruther, OP, *The Seminary Priests, Vol. 1, Elizabethan 1558–1603* (Gateshead: Northumberland Press Ltd), pp. v–vi.

CHAPTER 4

'A very superstitious Papist'

BEFORE ROGER RETURNED TO ENGLAND he was physically, intellectually and spiritually armed to engage in the battle that lay ahead of him. He had renounced his patrimony in order to do this. He had been prepared in the seminaries abroad to carry the work of the Counter-Reformation forward and to restore Catholicism to England and, if necessary, die in the attempt.

As a boy growing into a man abroad, especially as a scholar with a 'talent for controversy', he would have spent a great deal of time engaged in understanding the mind-set of the hierarchy of the new Church in England. By doing this he would have prepared himself for the time that lay ahead, which he describes later as 'entering the listes'.

Many leading Protestant churchmen had spent time in exile in northern Europe during the reign of Mary Tudor. Here they had come under the influence of the followers of the philosophies of Zwingli, Calvin and Luther. Heady with their new, intellectualised faith they returned to England when Elizabeth acceded to the throne. By the end of the sixteenth century the Queen, a traditionalist herself, could not find a man of her persuasion qualified to be a Bishop who would be acceptable to her Protestant advisers, especially the chief amongst them, William Cecil. There was no one to be found who was not in prison or exile who did not subscribe to this new intellectualised faith. They claimed that it had its basis in the early Church and the Scriptures which they had begun to freely interpret.

It may have been at Rheims that the young Roger, with his great facility for languages, began his work of translating from the Greek Theodoret's *Philotheus,* or *The Lives of the Fathers of the Syrian Desert.* Theodoret was a Bishop of Cyrrhus (c.393–c.458) and his work is described by the *Oxford Dictionary of the Christian Church* as 'one of the finest Christian apologies'. Roger's translation was published in St Omer, posthumously, in 1612. It is said to be extant, and there may be a copy at Stonyhurst with annotations by Roger in the margins, but this has not yet come to light. It must have been seen by one of the monks of Belmont Abbey because among the papers in the Archives is a translation of the Cadwallador Foreword. The arguments in the text are those of Roger based on Theodoret.[1]

There is much in the Foreword to indicate that Roger drew on the work of Theodoret to answer the religious questions of the day, particularly those arguments which were so prevalent at the time and related to the nature of the Early Church. It is by reading the Belmont translation of the Theodoret Foreword by Cadwallador that it is possible to understand the ardent, driven, intelligent reasoning that motivated him.

He starts by writing that he has prepared this translation of notable ancient history into English so that his reader may clearly see that the practice of the primitive Church in 'purer times' of Christianity was the same as 'that which we Catholics hold at the present day and quite contrary to the reformed faith of the Protestants'. He trusts that from reading Theodoret,

> it will plainly appear on which of the sides the Truth standeth. And that the Catholics have great reason to adventure both Lands and Life in defence of so undoubted and so ancient a Faith which is common to them with the Apostles and the Apostolic men, and which has been professed in all the Christian world, and delivered unto them from hand to hand, and finally they stand in possession to this present time, and will ever make their claim unto it.

Having discussed the rightness of his ancient Faith as described in the Apostles' Creed and handed down unchanged through the centuries from Christianity's earliest days, he grasps the nettle of the Scriptures.

Aidan Nichols, OP, in *The Panther and the Hind*[2] is helpful in explaining four of the sources which were the major influences on Protestant thinking. Guided by Nichols, it is possible to show how Roger answers them in his Introduction to Theodoret.

The first is the Wycliffe source which 'accepted the Bible as the only basis for the determination of Christian doctrine'. Roger writes in his Introduction about the need to consider Tradition, 'But in an history so ancient as this' (meaning his translation of the *Ecclesiastical History of Theodoret*) 'which being nearer to the times of the Apostles, might better hold what they held and taught, than we can now'.

The second of the four sources is the Erastian element which taught that every subject is bound to obey the king, an idea which comes from Romans 13, and begs the question of what to do if the king is theologically wrong.

The Lutheran element is the third source which has at the heart of its teaching salvation through faith alone. Luther struck at the basis of medieval piety: pilgrimages, the veneration of saints, works of penance, indulgences, intercessory masses and prayer for the dead. All of which the Council of Trent emphasised should continue.

The fourth source is the Reformed Element of which there is a great deal of interest to say, but for the purposes of the search for Roger Cadwallador it is easiest to reduce the Reformed Element to a belief in predestination, a low doctrine of the Eucharist, a root and branch opposition to Our Lady and the saints and a rejection of the Episcopacy. Not least there was a determination to create a godly city, based on the righteousness of the elect, rather than what Aidan Nichols describes as 'the untidy world of medieval Catholicism, where the royal power and the episcopal were imperfectly intermixed'.

Thus Theodoret, suggests Roger Cadwallador, might have been writing about the times in which he, the young Roger, lived, recording as Theodoret did the works of famous Bishops of the early Church as well as the persecutions raised by heretics and other tyrants, and:

> The constancy and resolution of Catholics, what heretics impugned the Church; and what Martyrs shed their blood to defend it, what Confessors either by written books or by miracles did confirm it: what famous Monks and Eremites then flourished either in Towns or Deserts. He also reporteth with what liberty of speech the Saints of those times rebuked the Tyrany of Princes and Potentates, whenever they intruded themselves into causes Ecclesiastical.

All this, writes Cadwallador, would cause Protestant adversaries to 'censure him for a very superstitious Papist'. Then Roger defines the Papacy:

> The (Early) Church ... had one supreme Pastor under Christ, whose sentence in matters of the Faith was to be accepted above all the rest ... who for his sovereign Authority is called Papa. That is Father and calls all other bishops his Sons and extendeth his jurisdiction into foreign countries.

He described the role of priests as 'such as offer sacrifice'. He wrote of the role of deacons, lectors and other orders of clergy and he wrote of religious orders. He touched on the single life, which Bishops led in those days.

Roger continually returned to the universality of the Catholic Faith from the beginning. There can be no doubt that he believed that it was the Church that Christ came to found and for which his death and burial was like the Seed falling into the ground. He describes churches to be found throughout Christendom in the time of Theodoret:

We read of fair and goodly Churches gilded with Gold, dedicated to the Service of God, consecrated and hallowed by Bishops, and Altars in them glittering with ornaments and wrought with gold and precious stones. And because as St Jerome saith (there can be) 'no Church which hath no Priests' (Sacerdotes). Priests were required to serve in the churches, for no other purpose (no doubt) but for the saying of Masses on those Altars, and ministering the Sacraments. In these churches also we find that there were relics of Saints and Miracles done by them, there were holy vestments for the clergy, Chalices and other vessels of Gold and silver. There was holy water and miracles done thereby. There were wax candles, prayers made for the dead, and to the Saints departed. There were fasting days, as Lent and Ember days, feasts as Christmas, Easter, other feasts of Martyrs. For proof whereof, I refer the reader to the work itself where he shall find mention made of these matters, almost in every Chapter.

The contrast with the Reformed Protestant Church in England is not to be missed. This from the *Stripping of the Altars* by Professor Eamon Duffy[3]:

In response to central diktat the altars were drawn down and the walls whited, windows broken or blotted out ... Veils and vestments, chalices and chests and hangings, the accumulation of generations of pious donations, were surrendered to the King's commissioners ... in most churches the altars were gone, the niches were empty.

The sense of disorientation, indeed desolation, felt by the traditional faithful is well expressed in an anonymous lament over the despoiled shrine of Our Lady at Walsingham, England's Nazareth. The poet portrays the fate of the shrine as an expression in miniature of the ravaging of England's spiritual landscape, 'while the shepherds [meaning the orthodox bishops] did sleep'. It finishes with this last poignant lament. The poem is attributed to the Earl of Arundel:

Oules do scrike where the sweetest himnes lately weer songe.
Toades and serpents hold their dennes wher the palmers did thronge.
Weepe, weepe O Walsingham, whose days are nights,
Blessings turned to blasphemies, holy deeds to dispites.
Sinne is wher our Ladie sate, heaven turned is to hell,
Sathan sites wher our Lord did swaye, Walsingham oh farewell.[4]

Notes

1   Belmont Abbey Archives.
2   A. Nichols, *The Panther and the Hind* (Edinburgh: T&T Clarke, 1994), pp. 1–36.
3   E. Duffy, *The Stripping of the Altars* (New Haven and London: Yale University Press, 2005), pp. 478–503.
4   Philip, Earl of Arundel, *The New Oxford Book of Sixteenth-Century Verse* (Oxford: OUP, 1991), pp. 550–551.

CHAPTER 5

The Missioner

ROGER CADWALLADOR, following his priesting, returned to work in the English Mission mainly in Herefordshire but also in the neighbouring counties of Monmouthshire and Worcestershire.

> He deservedly gained the character of a pious, prudent, and zealous missioner: and God was pleased to bless his labours with great success, in winning over many souls to Christ and his church especially among the poorer sort, for whose comfort, and spiritual assistance, he spared no pains, night or day; usually performing his journies on foot.[1]

This paragraph from Challoner's *Memoirs* is quoted at the beginning of almost every article about Blessed Roger. It is very important in the search for the Marches' hidden saint.

In 1585 the missionaries were declared traitors by English law. If a priest was arrested and brought before a magistrate he was forced to answer the so-called 'Bloody Question'. This question asked, 'If the Pope and the King of Spain landed in England, for whom would you fight?' An impossible question for most priests who were Englishmen and preferred their own Queen Elizabeth to King Philip and would be unhappy to see any of their flock at the sharp end of a Spaniard's pike or to witness the horrors of the French Wars of Religion visited on their own native land. No satisfactory answer had been devised and a steady stream of brave and honourable priests continued to suffer the agonies of a traitor's death.

With the return of the missionaries, the number of recusants grew in the Marches and presumably a fringe of those sympathetic to the Faith but not included in official statistics. Another time of growth in recusancy occurred toward the end of Elizabeth's reign when it was hoped that the new monarch would have a more tolerant policy towards Catholicism.

When Roger returned to England, Catholicism had developed an aristocratic flavour.[2] Priests educated abroad in colleges like Cardinal Allen's Douai or by the Jesuits came, almost without exception, from the families of the gentry. When they came back to the English mission they passed in disguise from the shelter of one great house to another. In this way they could remain concealed. Because of this a large number of their converts came from the families, servants and tenants of Catholic squires.

That is why it is remarkable that Roger Cadwallador put his energy and intellect at the service of the poor and why it is important in this search to stress Bishop Challoner's accolade:

> Winning over many souls to Christ and his church especially among the poorer sort for whose comfort, and spiritual assistance, he spared no pains, night or day; usually performing his duties on foot.

Members of the poor Catholic community were classed as vagrants and the undeserving poor. Challoner suggests that Cadwallador the priest and the yeoman farmer's son would have fed the poor both materially, for 'their comfort' and spiritually, which he calls 'spiritual assistance'. In the part of Roger Cadwallador's parish close to the Golden Valley there was a very long established community of hundreds of impoverished smallholders who lived in ugly, tumbledown mud huts. Although they were native Herefordians, they were amongst the poorest of the poor and were Roman Catholics.

Conditions in England at that time were appalling.[3] At the end of the sixteenth century there was a series of disastrous harvests.

Almost inevitably plague[4] followed fast on the heels of famine. In times of crop failure shipments of foreign grain were brought into the towns and stored in granaries. Rats, which host the flea carrying the plague, were imported with the grain. In the country-side the rat population was less of a threat because it was scattered over a large rural area, but storing grain in the towns meant that country rats migrated to the towns bringing the plague with them. Those who were fortunate enough to have the means to escape plague-ridden communities moved to safe houses in the country or abroad. There was no escape for the poor.

Thousands of people in England were unable to get work, and sold everything they had, even their bed straw. They were reduced to eating dogs, or horse meat which had been set aside for the hounds. Extreme hunger and suffering were to continue for thirty years and this was especially true of the Marches. In 1637 the county sheriff of Herefordshire was to declare, 'For so small a circuit as this shire contains there are not in the kingdom a greater number of poor people.'

The cost of fighting the Spanish Armada had to be met by stringent taxation when money was already in short supply. The Catholic community whom Challoner describes as 'the poorer sort' was destitute to the point of starvation and at the end of the line when it came to aid because of their Catholic religion. It was a religion they shared with the hated Spanish and made them scape-goats for the hardships that the nation was suffering.

The Crown had not profited greatly from the suppression of the monasteries.[5] It had taken on not only the properties of the monasteries but also an obligation to meet a fairly hefty pension bill. Most monks had pensions that barely covered their basic needs and nuns were even less generously treated and were forced onto the charity of friends and relations or, not uncom-monly, into marriage. If the Crown had retained possession of monastic properties until all of the pensioners died off it might have accrued some revenue. However properties were sold at the market rate and the money used to fund very expensive wars

against France and Scotland in the 1540s, and to stave off royal
bankruptcy for a single generation. There was no question of
there being any money for the Church in England, of which
Henry had made himself head.

Taxes for the relief of the sick and the poor were met with opposition according to the *Agrarian History of England and Wales*.
Hardly any of the middle-class clergy in ordinary livings had
private incomes but they were obliged to maintain a certain state
and hospitality on their inadequate funds. They were often
querulous and persistent in their expostulations and took what
they could by way of fines and short-term gains. Each benefice
included a certain amount of land but the clergy had no experience
of the management needed for it to prosper. Sadly the example of
some of the Bishops was a degeneration into avarice and corrup-
tion, and allegations of simony and greed were often made and not
without some justification both before and after the Reformation.

It might be argued that before the Reformation monasticism
had its share of villains but there can be no doubt that by its eradi-
cation the country lost its 'Welfare State'. Monasteries prospered
because they were in the hands of good stewards. In addition *The
Agrarian History* says, after the Dissolution, the important
question might be that:

> The dead hand of the Church over so considerable a part of the
> country had a stifling effect on agricultural experiment. The day
> had long since gone when the monasteries produced crops and
> stock for the market.[6]

Church courts were held in larger churches and parishioners
were called to answer charges or present cases in front of a judge,
scribe and various others. Churchwardens were meant to present
lists of offenders, such as those who secretly married outside the
established Church, clandestine baptisms, fornication and failure
to attend church, to an 'apparitor' who would summon the
offenders. Punishments varied from a warning to penances and

fines, then finally to excommunication. The scribe noted this down in church court books, an excellent, if fusty, source for historians in search of evidence of recusancy.

It is also possible to ascertain the social status of individuals in each parish from the names of individuals shown on rolls of parchments recording Lay Subsidies. These were national taxes on all who had above a certain amount of land or property. They were paid to the king and collected by a relatively high status individual who would have received a fee for his trouble.

Roger Cadwallador would not have been able to give the poor of his parish the support they needed without the charity of better-off Catholic families. Amongst the gentry there was hardly a significant Marches family that did not have its recusant branch. These were the people who provided him with material support and a network of 'safe houses'. So effective were they that Roger was able to continue his ministry for years while infuriating the Bishop of Hereford who was writing regularly to Lord Salisbury to complain about him and his parishioners and begging for something to be done about them.

In the North of the county, Roger said Mass at Winsley House at Hope under Dinmore and at Wintercott near Ivington,[7] places associated with the Berringtons, a well-known recusant family. He encouraged one of the Berrington sons, George, to go to the English College at Valladolid. Later, when George returned to the English Mission in Hereford, the Bishop (Godwin, 1617–1633) recorded that he was unable to capture him. He said, 'I have laid all the gynnes [traps] I can think of but without success.' George Berrington was a Benedictine as were others, including Dom Walter William Kemble and the Appellant martyr, Robert Drurie, who appears often in these pages.

Drurie was a Secular priest but appears to have become a Benedictine. If he did, it would have been very early in the second flowering of the English Benedictines, which began in 1607, the year of his martyrdom. A contemporary record suggests he may have been martyred with his Benedictine seal on his person, and wearing the Benedictine habit.[8]

The re-founding of the English Benedictines is closely associated with a young lawyer, David Baker, later, Dom Augustine OSB, of Abergavenny, a short distance from Hereford. Dom Augustine's biographer, Dom Leander Prychard, recorded a meeting in 1603 with the Appellant and associate of Roger Cadwallador, William Watson, near Hay-on-Wye. Watson was on the run after the Bye plot. Much is unknown because of the dangers of those penal times but there is evidence of the new growth of the Benedictines in the Marches and there are several Cadwallador connections. The Scropes of Stretton Court were linked with Roger as well as families in Hereford city itself where he was known to have said Mass.

Chief amongst the Herefordshire recusant families and linked to each other by marriage were the Bodenhams, Baskervilles and Morgans who were known supporters of Blessed Roger. Sir Charles Morgan, who was related to almost every notable recusant family in Herefordshire, allowed the Mass to take place at Treville Park, Arkston and Whitfield close by. These locations were all part of the area in which Roger Cadwallador worked. 'Treville' occurs so frequently in the search for Roger Cadwallador that it begins to appear that it may have had the same significance to the Seculars as the Cwm did to the Jesuits.

The Kemble family, George living at Pembridge Castle, Welsh Newton, and his brother John at Llangarren, are recorded on a recusancy list of 1604. These two, the fathers and grandfathers of at least five priests, including St John Kemble, may have been known to Roger. They were deeply committed Catholics living in the area in which he ministered. Dom Walter William Kemble, OSB, probably an older brother of St John Kemble, was born in Herefordshire in the area served by Roger. He was professed at St Gregory's, 1 October 1620. He served on the Mission in the southern Benedictine province and was buried at Fownhope, near Hereford on 23 October 1633, forty-six years before his brother's martyrdom.

There were a growing number of Jesuit converts congregating in the southern end of the area which Roger worked. Father Persons, the Prefect of the English Jesuit mission, sent Father Robert Jones[9] to serve their needs. Father Jones arrived in the country in 1595 and by 1605 had established an organization, centred in Monmouthshire and extending along the Marches where there was an uneasy relationship with the secular clergy, including Roger, but Robert Jones was to do him a service at the end of his life. He was known as the 'fyrebrand of alle' and was so called because he was suspected of subversive political activities by the sheriff in Herefordshire. Father Jones appears to have been a good priest as witnessed by a letter urging Aquaviva, his Superior in Rome, to send only 'truly discreet, prudent, mortified, humble and patient' men, who would be Jesuits, to the Welsh and English Mission. This may have been one explanation of why the Jesuit mission flourished in the Marches.

The evidence is that the Catholic people of his parish and other clergy loved Roger Cadwallador and protected him. They were so effective at doing this that when danger threatened they spirited him away and hid him, and so he was able to continue his ministry for seventeen years until he was captured. There were other trusted individuals who formed a net of support around him including James Coles, the clerk to the priest. He also had loyal friends including his 'trustid John of Hereford'. 'Trustid John' may have been John Harley, a physician. The family doctor would have been especially valuable to the organisation of any parish because of his ability to pass unremarked from home to home.

The role of women in this network of support was crucial. Robert Bennet, a protégé of Sir Robert Cecil, had been appointed Bishop of Hereford in 1603 in order to deal with Catholic intransigence in the diocese. His preferred method was by the use of commissions sent by the King, the Bishop of London and Cecil. In one of Bishop Bennet's letters requesting a commission, he refers to 'the lawless ladies of Herefordshire'.

How angry the haughtiness of these county ladies must have made the Bishop who appears to have had a very high opinion of his own self-worth. The collection of fines imposed on recusants depended on those who maintained the law and in Herefordshire the lawless ladies were closely related to those in official positions and who would have been responsible for paying the fines and so were not pressed too hard.

The Lady Bridget Bodenham, a daughter of Sir Humphrey Baskerville of Eardisley, was found by the Bishop of Hereford to be imperious and quarrelsome and he expostulated that she 'countenanced all priests and recusants'. She was married to Sir Roger Bodenham who was a Papist but, because he was subject to the law, had to be more circumspect than she. Another woman, Lady Sibyl Seabourne, was married to John Seabourne, another well-known Catholic supporter of Roger Cadwallador, who was the landlord of a large area in which the priest ministered. Lady Sibyl was unusual in being named in 1604 as one of the principal and most dangerous recusants in the county and she would have definitely been counted as one of the lawless ladies.

There were other women, some of whom were supporters of the Jesuits in Herefordshire, who were equally, if not more brave and just as prepared to stand up to the Bishop. The Jesuits attracted people from outside the Marches. This influx of people from the Jesuit congregations in other counties settled around The Darrow, Llanrothal and the Cwm. These women and their families were at greater risk than some of the native Herefordians who had the tacit support of their wealthy male relatives.

A feature of many Catholic women in Herefordshire was their faithfulness to their religion and their quiet courage. In a letter from prison Roger Cadwallador wrote the following which has been transcribed from his original Latin using code names for the recipients and in which he writes of an unnamed woman's

hard work and devoted effort. I will not cease from remembering her and the others through whose support, blessed be God, I have no need of any earthly comfort. I bestow good wishes from the bottom of my heart as much on her as on my remaining brothers.

There were women who were less well-to-do than the lawless ladies and took care not to be known to the authorities and so were not counted officially as recusants. However they were crucial to the preservation of their priest and were an essential part of the supportive network which kept safe those of their families who had a more public role. Perhaps the most important thing was that they nurtured the next generation by teaching and living the Catholic Faith at a time when this took enormous courage. In those penal times the Roman Catholic laity shared with their priests a faith which was like a seal pressed onto the wax of their souls.

Notes

1   R. Challoner, *Memoirs of Missionary Priests and Other Catholics of Both Sexes That have Suffered Death in England on Religions Accounts from the Year 1577–1684* (Philadelphia: John T. Green, 1839), pp. 21–27.

2   A.G. Dickens, *The English Reformation* (Chatham, Kent: Batsford, 1989), pp. 367–369.

3   H.P.R. Finberg (ed.), *The Agrarian History of England and Wales, Vol. 4, 1500–1640* (Cambridge: Cambridge University Press, 1967), p. 439.

4   *Ibid.*, pp. 356, 593, 633.

5   G.W.O. Woodward, *The Dissolution of the Monasteries* (Caterham & Crawley: Garrod and Lofthouse Int. Ltd, 1974), pp. 22–24.

6   Finberg, *The Agrarian History of England and Wales*, p. 356.

7   N.C. Reeves, *The Parish of St Ethelbert, Leominster* (Leominster: Norman C. Reeves, 1972), pp. 33–34.

8   http://en.wikipedia.org/wiki/Robert_Drury_(priest)

9   T.M. McGoog, 'Robert Jones', *Oxford Dictionary of National Biography*, vol. 30 (Oxford: Oxford University Press, 2004), p. 621.

CHAPTER 6

The Desire for a Bishop

ROGER CADWALLADOR was aware of the history of the early Church, and his work on the translation of Theodoret with his powerful Introduction appears to be an exposition of his own Catholic thinking. Working on the scriptural translations while a student in Rheims would have given him a deep familiarity with the events of Christ's Resurrection. He would have studied the way in which the history of these events was passed down by the original eyewitnesses. He would have understood the way in which this witness was at the heart of the historical continuity which is the Apostolic Succession. It would have been his contention that the Church believes the Good News and does not despair in the face of death because the Truth has been received through the Apostolic Succession. Bishops have declared so and they are to be trusted because they are the appointed successors of the original Apostles who had met and talked with the risen Christ. This has resonances today in the Catechism.[1]

A Bishop is integrated into the Episcopal College to share with the Pope the care for all the churches and he receives the offices of teaching, sanctifying and ruling. In addition the Bishop is to care for a church in a specific diocese. The Council of Trent had laid stress on the pastoral duties of the Bishop who was to be the visible head and focus for unity for a particular area of the Church. Assisted by his own priests and deacons he would fulfil the office of shepherd of an identified flock.

Christ appointed his Apostles to rule in his name. He said, 'he who hears you, hears me'. In their turn the Apostles appointed successors of their own by the laying on of hands. Blessed Roger showed in his Introduction to Theodoret that, looking back on history, the orders of bishops, priests and deacons have existed from the earliest days of the Church. The lives and work of bishops on the continent would have made him aware of the essential contribution of the episcopacy to the Church.

One of the best known episcopal figures of the Counter-Reformation was St Charles Borromeo, Cardinal Archbishop of Milan, who died in 1568.[2] At the end of the sixteenth century and beginning of the seventeenth century a *Life of St Charles* was being circulated in England. There were reports from English Catholics returning from abroad, such as the Jesuit martyr St Edmund Campion, about St Charles Borromeo's philosophy and work. In the early days of the Society of Jesus, St Charles had been a supporter of the Order. Those who desired a Bishop would also have been aware that St Charles had been prepared to risk his own life as he had been the target of an assassination attempt.

In these ways, and because of the time he had spent abroad, Roger would have been aware of the effect of the reforms of St Charles who, although filled with self-sacrificing zeal, was not so aesthetic that he could not still enjoy the occasional game of billiards. He managed the wayward behaviour of his clergy with great tact and understood and provided for their need for education and supported them in their parishes. His intense pastoral activity, his investment in his clergy and his self-emptying works of charity were a pattern of the episcopacy for anywhere, including England.

St Francis de Sales,[3] who was an almost exact contemporary of Roger, became Bishop of Geneva in 1602, the year of the Protestation of Allegiance. He came from a wealthy family who did not support his vocation to be a priest. After being educated by the Jesuits, he had become a missionary in the most dangerous of circumstances. He once had a price on his head, had been attacked by wolves, threatened by assassins, and beaten by angry mobs. He had been sent to win Calvinists back to the Catholic faith, teaching the Catholic belief in free will as opposed to Calvin's theory of predestination.

To guide the faithful from heresies is an example of another duty of a Bishop. His role is to maintain orthodoxy, as it were, to keep the fences in order to preserve the flock. St Francis de Sales did this by his great ability as a communicator, both in his writing of popular books on theology and by his preaching. He was a humanist with a deep love of his fellow men and women. His total commitment to the Faith was a position he reached after a long period of wrestling with the doubt that God loved him. He combined gentleness and understanding of humanity's troubles and temptations with a deep-rooted hope of salvation. He had no time for the doctrine of predestination and the hopelessness and despair which it engenders. He possessed qualities that hard-pressed missionary priests in England, struggling to revive the drooping spirits of their flock, must have desired in a Bishop. Roger Cadwallador may not have known St Francis de Sales' motto but it is easy to see that he would have approved of its courageous sentiments. 'Go simply. If you have any fears, say to your soul that the Lord will provide for you. Trust in him, depend on his providence. Fear nothing.'

Perhaps the Bishop who had most relevance for Roger was Dr Thomas Watson[4] who had grown to maturity in the dreadful days of Henry VIII and died in the Faith in the final years of Elizabeth's reign. Because of this it is helpful to look in detail at his life which must have impacted on Roger and Catholicism in England at the time.

As a young man in the reign of Henry VIII, Dr Watson had walked the tightrope between treason and conviction from which so many were to fall to their deaths. Dr Watson, in his early years, might well have fitted the description given by Calvin to those who, in those vicious, unforgiving days, professed a secret adherence. Calvin called them 'Nicodemists', after the Pharisee Nicodemus who visited Christ under cover of darkness. It was an approach adopted by many Englishmen, as the alternative was death or exile at best.

Forced to swear the 'Oath of Allegiance' to Henry VIII which included a promise to forsake the Bishop of Rome, Dr Watson wrote a five-act play, *Absalom*, which was unpublished and lay undiscovered in the British Museum until 1963. The play was written to describe his true feelings but also gives a fascinating picture of the causes and effects of Henry VIII's Protestant Reformation by an eyewitness who was loyal to the Pope. The first four acts look at parallels with what had happened so far in Henry's England, merging biblical events with events taking place all around England. The last act describes Dr Watson's conviction that health in the shape of the restoration of the Catholic faith would be achieved.

Bishop Watson's play, *Absalom*, is also helpful in understanding the falling away from the Faith at the time of Henry VIII and who should be blamed. Bishop Watson hoped that one day Catholicism would return. His is a very different opinion from that, recorded earlier, of the *Catholic Encyclopedia*, which blames 'Papal domination' for the nation's loss of faith in the Church. The play has added value because it was written by a Roman Catholic Bishop who lived through Henry VIII's Reformation.

The play begins with a prince, Absalom (representing Henry VIII), quarrelling with his father, David (who represents the Pope), about the relationship of Absalom's brother with a particular princess. Absalom demands a specific ruling from David which is refused. When Absalom acts in defiance of his father, David censures him. Infuriated, Absalom begins to undermine and then deny his father's authority. The innocent people of the kingdom are dismayed and forced to take sides. Absalom resorts to decrees, threats, intimidation and executions. Unrestrained by paternal authority, he brooks no opposition and he does whatever he likes.

In the play David is identified as God's elect. He is the undisputed authority and focus of unity for the diverse tribes of Israel. He is holy and pious and he wants to help Absalom, whom he loves, but he cannot. The play is not uncritical of David's weakness but the people revere him and his divine office as 'Holy Father' of God's people. Absalom is portrayed as David's once-devoted son. Now if his every whim is not indulged he flies into a rage so that even his ministers go in fear of him. The play warns that Absalom's pride, which cannot be curbed, will be his downfall. David now presides over the Old Jerusalem and Absalom over the New Jerusalem. Absalom violently usurps his father's place, seeing his father's hesitation because of his love for his son as weakness. The parallels in Dr Watson's play with the Dissolution are easy to see.

Using dramatic licence he now departs from the biblical story. Absalom sacks David's temples, expelling their guardians, looting their possessions and destroying their altars. They are based on events which Dr Watson had recently witnessed. The guardians are appalled and helpless and unable to stop the ruthless plundering of the monasteries, guilds, shrines and chantry chapels to fill Absalom's (Henry's) own treasury, fund his rebellion and secure his position.

As the play moves towards its conclusion, even those closest to Absalom are appalled by his ferocity. He turns on these as the king turned on Wolsey, Fisher, More and Cromwell. Disenchanted, his subjects begin to convert back to David and start to join those who had gone into hiding. The paranoid Absalom, trusting no-one, begins a relentless persecution of those loyal to David. The play then looked to the future. There is a final battle as is recorded in the Old Testament and David is the victor but movingly aches for the loss of his beloved son. The play is not uncritical of David's weakness but the conclusion is that his victory is inevitable.

Thomas Watson had emerged as a champion and preacher of the 'Old Faith' while at St John's College, Cambridge, under the Chancellor, John Fisher. He worked side by side with Stephen Gardiner, the Bishop of Winchester, and became his chaplain. During the last two years of Henry VIII's reign, Watson, with Gardiner, worked hard to keep the Church in England Catholic at a time when Lutheranism was on the increase. Given the character of this sick and dying king, who in the last months of his life ordered the execution of three Papists for questioning his royal supremacy and the burning of three Lutherans for questioning his Catholic doctrine, this was no easy task.

When Edward VI succeeded to the throne, Watson was arrested and thrown into the Fleet prison but was later released. Throughout those notoriously difficult days Watson had bided his time, never gainsaying his faith, but infuriating the Protestant opposition by what they saw as his prevarication.

Mary Tudor acceded to the throne on the death of her frail half-brother. Thomas Watson was chosen by her to formally announce her intention to restore England to the Catholic Faith. The main tenet of Watson's argument for Catholic orthodoxy was 'the Mass which is the Sacrifice of the New Testament'. In addition he believed that the Early Fathers, the Doctors of the Faith and the Councils of the Church witnessed to the truth of Catholic Eucharistic teaching. His main task during the reign of Mary Tudor was the restoration of Catholic doctrine, customs and liturgy. In addition he was charged with attempting to recover the valuables, property and land plundered during the previous two reigns.

In 1557 Thomas Watson was consecrated Bishop of Lincoln. His was the last ever appointment to that post to be made by papal bull. He was one of the queen's most celebrated spokesmen but even at the most severe and bloody period of Mary's campaign against Protestantism there was not a single execution in his diocese, which was the largest in the land. When Mary died in November 1558, Watson was sent to the Tower and by June 1559 he had been tried, found guilty of treason, deprived of his bishopric and given a life sentence. Dr Watson's reaction when the Pope excommunicated Elizabeth in 1570 was to be less than delighted and to regret that it might create greater hardship for Catholics which it inevitably did. The excommunicated sovereign was now in danger of officially sanctioned assassination and anti-papal sentiment would become overtly anti-Catholic hatred.

In 1580 the Bishop of Ely had been ordered to turn his palace, Wisbech Castle, into an internment centre for Catholics. Wisbech Castle was originally a motte and bailey castle built by William the Conqueror to fortify Wisbech in the Fenland area of Cambridgeshire. In Tudor times the rebuilt Castle became a notorious prison.

Dr Watson was one of the first of eight prisoners to be interred in Wisbech Castle. When he was transferred to the Castle in 1580 he had already been a prisoner for more than twenty years. There is evidence that he found that he was among friends, including the last Abbot of Westminster, Abbot Fakenham, whom he had known as an undergraduate at Cambridge. Amongst the small group there were former Marian priests as well as newly-arrived seminary priests and Jesuits, all of whom accepted his authority. He appears to have exercised an episcopal ministry of gentleness and harmony 'in vinculis'. He died in Wisbech Castle in 1584 and lies in an unmarked grave somewhere in the churchyard of Wisbech Parish Church. Following his death, without dedicated episcopal leadership, the different threads of Catholicism in Wisbech began to unravel. In his lifetime, under his leadership he had held them together, even influencing his gaolers.

Notes

1   The Catholic Bishops' Conference of England and Wales, *Compendium, Catechism of the Catholic Church* (London: C.T.S., 2006), pp. 11–16, 162, 167, 174–176, 187.
2   T. Cowan, *The Way of the Saints* (New York: Berkley, 1998), pp. 109–110.
3   *Ibid.*, pp. 170–171.
4   'Thomas Watson (Bishop of Lincoln)': wikipedia.org/wiki/Thomas_ Watson_(bishop_of_Lincoln).

CHAPTER 7

The Wisbech Stirs

HE POLITICS AND THE personalities involved in the
Wisbech Stirs are relevant to the search for Roger Cadwallador. As the documents held by the Benedictine monks at
Belmont Abbey show, Roger was later involved in both the Archpriest Controversy and the Protestation of Allegiance which
followed. As the Stirs are seminal to these events, it is necessary to
look at their place in Roger's history in some depth.

While Bishop Thomas Watson exercised a benign episcopal
authority, and numbers were not as great as they later became, the
situation in Wisbech Castle was tolerable. A decree was passed in
the year of his death, 1584, limiting the number of prisoners to
twenty. At first discipline was strict with the prisoners being kept
locked in separate rooms, except at meal times and for half an
hour's exercise before dinner and supper.

Thomas Watson had died in 1584. He was the last Catholic
Bishop in England to command general allegiance and after his
death the organisation of the clergy began slowly to collapse. The
last member of the ancient hierarchy was Goldwell, Bishop of St
Asaph, who died in 1585. After that, Cardinal Allen exercised an
informal jurisdiction with the agreement of the Pope and with the
common consent of the 300 or so missionary priests, but this was
episcopal government from abroad and depended on the personal
charisma of Cardinal Allen.

After the Armada in 1588, the number of prisoners rose to
thirty-five and, under a relatively benign gaoler, there was a relax-
ation in the close surveillance that had existed previously.[1] This

meant that servants were allowed to be kept, visitors to be admitted and food to be sent in by friends. Priests were allowed to go into the town. The prisoners paid twelve shillings a month for their keep. For two years the castle became a kind of ecclesiastical college with deep and prayerful theological debates. It also became a place of pilgrimage for the Roman Catholic laity.

The Keeper of the castle at that time was Thomas Grey, but in 1590 his treatment of the prisoners was reported to be lax and a commission was sent to investigate. His daughter Ursula had forsaken her Puritan upbringing and had been received into the Faith. The commission made some harsh recommendations which were strictly enforced. The castle building was strengthened. Townsmen who were considered trustworthy were appointed to assist, almost to guard, the keeper who was not allowed to leave the castle without a special dispensation. Communication with the outside was severely restricted, visitors were only to be allowed by special permission and incoming letters were censored. Inside the castle, the original policy of separating the prisoners except at mealtimes was reintroduced and they were not allowed out of the castle grounds. Food was reduced to the meagre diet of the notorious Fleet prison. For this existence the prisoners were now made to pay in a week more than they had paid in a month.

Plans of the castle at that time show that the area of the prison was small, cramped and insanitary.[2] The numbers incarcerated meant that existing problems were bound to be exacerbated by the stringent conditions imposed by the commission. The Wisbech Stirs saw the breakdown of collegiality between the Regular clergy and the Secular clergy. Secular priests are not subject to or bound by a religious rule because these priests do not belong to, or live in, a religious order. The majority of missionary priests in England were Secular priests. This is in contrast to the Regulars who were subject to a rule imposed by a religious order. The Regulars were the Jesuits and their collaborators.

The religious order of the Society of Jesus was founded by St Ignatius Loyola and formally approved by Pope Paul III in 1540.

Originally the aim of the Society was the defeat of the Mohammedans. It was organised, uniform and united, following a religious rule and relying on alms. The Jesuits had had their critics from the beginning. Soon after the Council of Trent, St Philip Neri, the Oratorian, whom the Romans loved, said that when he was faced with a dilemma he would discover what Ignatius Loyola, the founder of the Jesuits, had decided and do the opposite. It is to the credit of the Church that there is room for both points of view and St Philip Neri and St Ignatius Loyola were canonised on the same day in the same year.

Later, the lowest point in Jesuit history was brought about by its suppression in 1770–1773. They were deserted by everyone they considered their friend, including the Pope, and they lost everything they had built up. Then they were saved by the action of their former enemies at the Russian and the Prussian courts. The Jesuits were to emerge from this humiliation with their faith deepened and strengthened.

Today the Society is established world-wide and famous for its work in education, mission and amongst the poor. In this new century the wheels of time have turned full circle and we have a Jesuit Pope, Francis. On the Pontiff's first Maundy Thursday in 2013, only weeks after his election, he knelt in front of a Moslem woman to wash her feet.

The rule that demanded the reliance on charity meant that a Jesuit, especially those who lived on the edge of the court in Elizabethan times, usually lived in the household of a wealthy benefactor. Some of the Jesuits had benefactors who appear to have been implicated in plots against the Elizabethan throne which exacerbated the fear-fed paranoia, so much a feature of the time.

Antonia Fraser, in her book *The Gunpowder Plot*,[3] says that 'the brilliant intellectual Jesuits were envied by the Appellants for the civilised lives they led in the great houses that nurtured them'.

The records show that two scions of the 'great houses' that nurtured the Jesuits, Robert Catesby and Francis Tresham, were imprisoned for a time in Wisbech Castle, possibly at the time of the Armada or at a period when the ageing queen was thought to be in danger of death from illness and the succession was an issue. Robert Catesby, not Guy Fawkes, is generally accepted to be the instigator of the Gunpowder Plot. The *Catholic Encyclopedia* quotes the nineteenth-century historian Tierney in relation to this act of treason as,

> the contrivance of half a dozen persons of desperate fortunes, who by that means, brought odium upon the body of Catholics, who have ever since laboured under the weight of calumny, though no way concerned.

Robert Catesby, born in 1573, was related to several staunchly Catholic families including the Treshams, Vauxs, Monteagles and Habingtons. His mother was Anne Throckmorton. His father had been imprisoned and fined many, many times as a recusant and on one occasion appeared in the Star Chamber for supporting one of the most attractive of Jesuit martyrs, Edmund Campion. Later, with the approval of Queen Elizabeth, Catesby's father had been charged with the task of founding a Catholic colony in America, a plan which he abandoned in the face of Spanish opposition but is illustrative of the ambivalence that existed in the treatment of recusants. The state of Maryland was eventually established by George Calvert, 1st Lord Baltimore, at the time of Charles I in 1629, as a refuge for English Catholics. The 'Maryland Toleration Act' was the first law ever to guarantee the right to worship regardless of denomination.

Robert Catesby is thought to have attended the Douai College, then located at Rheims, in about 1586. Although younger than Roger Cadwallador by four or five years and embedded, as he may well have been, with the Jesuits, their paths might have crossed. What they studied in Rheims, however, appears to have been very different because it is thought that it was at Douai that Catesby learnt the art of casuistry from a book by the Jesuit Martin Azpilcueta which was being used in the schools. Casuistry is the employment of clever, but unsound, moral theology to allow a normally forbidden course of action. This may explain his resolution regarding the absolute morality of his opposition to the crown and his unwavering justification of the Gunpowder Plot.

Catesby was baptised as an Anglican and married to a wealthy Protestant, whom he loved dearly and grieved for when she died relatively young. These were by no means unusual compromises with Protestantism. He remained active in the Catholic, and particularly the Jesuit, cause throughout his life. He sheltered Jesuit priests and their relatives including the mother of Father Robert Persons. History shows that oppressive regimes which destroy the fortunes of one generation appear to affect the attitudes of the succeeding generation, causing anger and frustration which result in acts of anarchy, violence and terrorism. We live in troubled times ourselves and see the effect of unfairness and oppression on groups of the young and disaffected both abroad and in our own country. So often they react in a way which is a counsel of despair and do great harm to what is right and just in their own cause as well as tainting the innocent, appearing to learn nothing from the past and damaging the future.

Catesby was a glamorous figure, part of the outer circle that surrounded the court and noted to be always accompanied by a priest. While younger and more impressionable priests fell under his spell, leading Jesuits deplored his involvement with activities such as the rebellion of the Earl of Essex against the Queen, for which he was imprisoned and fined. Catesby was zealous and successful in persuading others into the faith, or at least his version of it. His dangerous charisma was such that he was to cause more damage to the English priesthood than anyone else of his day.

The Gunpowder Plotters were directly responsible for the deaths of some who were found guilty by association, like Father Henry Garnet and Father Edward Oldcorne, who were both Jesuits. It is possible to trace a direct line of increasing doubt and fear relating to Catholicism, flowing from the Gunpowder Plot which led to the deaths of Roger Cadwallador and Robert Drurie, and eventually to the martyrdom of our local Saint, the elderly, gentle, John Kemble.

John Kemble, a Secular priest, was executed in Hereford at a time when Titus Oates, one of the most unpleasant men in history, was trying to enforce the removal of the Jesuits from the Cwm, Llanrothal. The Jesuits escaped easily but John Kemble waited in his home in Pembridge Castle, refusing to abscond, and was arrested, tried and executed for his priesthood. St John Kemble's mortal remains are said to lie in the churchyard at Welsh Newton. His hand, recovered at the time of his execution in Hereford in 1679 and kept safe by the Jesuits, is in a beautiful reliquary above the Lady Chapel altar in the south aisle of the church of St Francis Xavier in Broad Street, Hereford. The catastrophic effects of the Gunpowder Plot lingered for centuries.

Another prisoner at Wisbech was Francis Tresham who was an almost exact contemporary of Roger Cadwallador. Older than his cousin, Robert Catesby, he was, nevertheless, the follower rather than the leader of the two. He, with Robert Catesby, was involved up to his ears in the Gunpowder Plot. Lacking the attractive attributes of his cousin he appears to have been a disaffected and unstable figure. He and his henchmen had been accused of a violent assault on the daughter of a tenant who owed him money and whose name he had substituted for his own on a privy-council warrant. He had other discreditable actions attributed to him including defrauding his own, more than generous, father of lands and money as well as defaming him to the King, James I and VI. He, too, was involved in the Essex rebellion with Catesby against the advice of senior Jesuit priests.

The presence of persons such as Robert Catesby and Francis Tresham must have added to the anxieties already present in Wisbech prison. In addition to the clerical antagonisms already existing between Jesuits and Seculars, it would have brought a darker and more political dimension to the Stirs.

The Stirs appear to have been further exacerbated by the death of Cardinal Allen, in 1594. His death was to have a disturbing effect on all English Catholics. Misery ran through the community like a sickness, causing discontent amongst the exiles and gradually affecting the seminaries and the clergy as well as the Catholic prisoners at home. Cardinal Allen was a charismatic figure who led by personal influence and there appears to have been no thought given to a successor.

In England, the Superior of the Jesuits before this time was Father William Weston.[4] Weston arrived in the prison at Wisbech in 1588. He had been sent to the English mission in 1584 at a time when there was no other Jesuit at liberty. He received Philip Howard, Earl of Arundel, into the Church, which was a considerable coup. He left an autobiography full of missionary adventures including details of the practice of exorcisms which he carried out with other impressionable missionary priests. Jesuit priests generally worked together in an almost military way. The exorcised were thought to have been suffering from diabolical possession, but it is now thought to have been hysteria (then called 'mother'). To the modern reader this may appear to be a curious mix of the medieval mind and Freudianism.

Older and wiser priests who thought it a dangerous practice were concerned about possible links with witchcraft and put a stop to the exorcisms which lasted only a year, before William Weston and several of those involved with him were imprisoned. Father Weston is often described in the articles one reads about him as fanatical and aesthetic but his personality certainly appears to have been charismatic. When he was imprisoned, his role as Superior of the English Jesuits passed to Henry Garnet, under the control of Robert Persons.

The leader of the Seculars was Christopher Bagshawe[5] who had recently converted to Roman Catholicism in 1582. Some years before, in 1574, he was involved in forcing the resignation of Father Robert Persons[6] when he was a fellow and tutor at Balliol College, Oxford. The reasons for Robert Persons' resignation are said to have been college quarrels as well as his strong Catholic leanings. It was only a year later, in 1575, that Father Persons, now in Rome, became a Jesuit.

Christopher Bagshawe was later involved in the Archpriest Controversy and was an Appellant. He was a 'new' man, in Catholic Counter-Reformation terms, who appears to have had very little love for Robert Persons. He was known for his quarrelsome nature and was expelled from the English College in Rome at a time when the Jesuits were in the ascendant, and transferred to the Sorbonne in Paris. Here he proceeded to become Doctor of Divinity and Doctor of the Sorbonne. The Sorbonne was later to figure in the Archpriest Controversy when those who were unhappy with the arrangement were accused of schism. It was William Weston who accused Christopher Bagshawe with Thomas Bluet, both later Appellants, of setting off the Stirs.

Doctor Bagshawe had an antipathy to leading Jesuits because of their political opinions and their strong preference for the Spanish throne which he felt would put the whole of the Catholic community in the country at risk. Robert Persons was particularly enamoured of the idea that the daughter of Philip II, the Archduchess Isabella, should succeed to the English throne. For a number of complex reasons, including her dislike of the idea, this was a fantasy, but Persons was not to be convinced.

The Seculars disliked the employment of Jesuitical equivocation, a doctrine of prevarication, which meant that the speaker's words could be taken two ways. A typical example is that of a Jesuit priest, who under severe pressure swore that he was 'no priest' meaning that he was not 'Apollo's priest at Delphos', and in addition, although he was much travelled abroad, he declared that he had never been beyond the sea, employing equivocation because he said that he meant that he had never been beyond the 'Indian seas'. This unfortunate Jesuit was in fear of his life, since to enter the country as a Roman Catholic priest from abroad was treason, for which the sentence was death. As it was, he was executed anyway.

Equivocation was seen by the Jesuits as a scrupulous way of

behaving by avoiding outright lies, as lying was prohibited by the Church. Father Henry Garnet, SJ,[7] had written a book about equivocation explaining how, and in what limited circumstances, it might be used.

Roger Cadwallador, with the other Seculars, rejected the practice of equivocation as 'in plain English' as they saw it, it was lying. The Appellants were saying this some years before the Gunpowder Plot when equivocation became a weapon to use against the Jesuits by their prosecutors, as it presented them as infiltrators from Rome with no allegiance to Britain. Equivocation, the Jesuits' persecutors sneered, was something that the Protestant martyrs Cranmer and Ridley would never have used to save their lives. Of course the situation of the Jesuit priests was very different from that of Cranmer and Ridley, but equivocation left the Jesuits vulnerable to ridicule and presented them as unpatriotic liars.

The Wisbech Stirs saw the Jesuits emerging as self-elected clerical leaders who wished for a more disciplined communal life. One of the strengths of the Jesuits is that they all live in community as regards food, apparel, lodging and recreation and all alike are bound by the rules of the Society. They saw the Seculars as intrinsically 'light-weight', failing to recognise the deep piety and loyalty to the Old Faith engendered in the seminaries. A little thought about the demand of those penal times would have made clear that the need for false identities and avoidance of the light of day was essential. My search has revealed how little is known of Blessed Roger and his brother Seculars, but if they had betrayed the great trust placed in them, we should have heard more than enough from their enemies.

Christopher Bagshawe arrived at Wisbech in 1593 when there had been a decrease of the strictness of the prison regime, and prisoners were allowed to live on alms supplied by Catholics and freedom of conversation was permitted. Catholic penitents were allowed to visit their confessors. This freedom allowed the prisoner priests to congregate.

Although the immediate cause of friction between the Regulars and Seculars was the keeping of fast days, this was only a symptom of the main problem. Weston's party wished for a more regulated community life, a religious rule, with a recognised authority to judge delinquencies which might involve quarrels and scandals. The problem was that in the restricted area of the prison it was impossible for two groups living separately to co-exist. The Regulars persisted and even dined apart. Bagshawe accused them of schism and denounced Weston as the cause. Weston was acting under the direction of Father Henry Garnet,[8] now the Jesuit Provincial, who had sanctioned the separate Regular life. Father Garnet's handling of the issue set off vehement protest from Bagshawe and his supporters. The protesters were intemperate in their language and it did the Seculars and their cause no credit.

After nine months of friction, two arbitrators, John Bavant and Alban Dolman, were called in, but one espoused one side and the other took the part of the other side. The quarrel continued for another five months until, in October 1595, John Mush and Dr Dudley were called in to arbitrate. John Mush was the confessor of the York martyr Margaret Clitheroe and was later involved on the Secular side with the Archpriest Controversy and with the Appellants. On this occasion Mush and Dudley arranged a compromise amid general rejoicing and the whole body agreed to live together by a definite rule. Also involved in the settlement was Father Henry Garnet, the Jesuits' Superior in England, whose letters to the prison were helpful in securing a resolution.

Weston and Bagshawe both emerge well from the Wisbech Stirs as the reconciliation was so warm and fraternal. If the Stirs had stopped there and not gone on to a subsequent quarrel, in 1598, about something completely different, it might have been remembered as a 'felix culpa'. If it had been allowed to continue, the hard won spirit of harmony and willingness to sacrifice private preference for the greater good might have helped to strengthen the Faith in England.

What better news could have greeted the newly-ordained Roger Cadwallador when he first set foot on English soil after so many years away from home? This outbreak of brotherly love must have appeared to be the best possible start to his missionary career.

Notes

1   'Wisbech, Recusants in the Castle', (British History, online, 2013).
2   'Wisbech Castle', (Wikipedia, 2012).
3   A. Frazer, *The Gunpowder Plot* (St Ives: Orion, 2002), pp. 52–56.
4   'William Weston', (Catholic Encyclopedia, online).
5   Christopher Bagshawe', (Catholic Encyclopedia, online).
6   M.L. Carrafiello, *Robert Parsons and English Catholicism, 1580–1610* (Google books, 1998).
7   'Henry Garnet', (Wikipedia, 2012).
8   'Henry Garnet', (Catholic Encyclopedia, online), current edition.

CHAPTER 8

The Archpriest Controversy

THE BELMONT ARCHIVES[1] contain the following information about Blessed Roger Cadwallador:

> During the seventeen years of his missionary career we hear from him from time to time. His name occurs in three separate lists of clergy who 'desire a bishop' and whilst a prisoner in Wisbech he sent his vote for those he thought most worthy.

From this we know that Roger was a prisoner for a time in Wisbech. Internment appears to have been almost a 'rite of passage' for missionary priests. Wisbech prison may have been viewed as a sort of ecclesiastical college, a place of growth and deepening of faith. We know from the Belmont documents that it put Roger at the heart of the events which were to shake the Roman Catholic Church in England.

No man is immortal and death abroad was to influence events at home, most notably the death of Cardinal Allen in 1594. A lack of foresight in Rome meant that there was no obvious successor, leaving the way open to a gathering storm of problems and discontent amongst English Catholics affecting the clergy, including the Catholic prisoners held at Wisbech and the seminaries. In the English College in Rome there was mounting discontent and protest. The Jesuit Father Robert Persons returned in 1597 and immediately restored order. Persons had general charge of and close contact with the Jesuit mission in England.

Robert Persons[2] was dynamic and forceful. It was Persons, with Cardinal Allen, who had been successful in organizing the English missionary enterprise between 1580 and 1581. At that time Jesuits, laymen and Secular priests cooperated in carrying out his plans and the results were encouraging. He may well have had good reason to see himself as Cardinal Allen's successor.

But Father Persons had not been so successful in the political arena. In 1582 he and Allen supported Mary Stuart in an ill-fated attempt by the Duke of Lennox to return her to Scotland against the wishes of the Scottish Kirk, and by acting as he did he set on edge the teeth of the majority of English people. Father Persons was dispatched to sue the King of Spain on Mary's behalf while others made approaches to the Pope. Pope Gregory responded positively to the diplomatic efforts in Mary's cause but King Philip did not, although he kept Persons dangling for two years before he gave his decision. King Philip II of Spain, infinitely powerful, liked to keep all his diplomatic irons in the fire.

Father Persons had chosen the wrong side, but this was understandable in view of the disapprobation of Elizabeth felt by the Pope and Cardinal Allen, as well as other leading Catholics abroad. Living away from England, he did not realise that there was a great deal of suspicion of Mary Stuart and his persistent support for her was not helpful. He had blessed the Spanish Armada as it sailed off to attack England. He began to be seen not as one who could deliver England from subjection but as someone who put Catholics at home at risk of persecution. Even worse, the Jesuits in England were beginning to be seen as untrustworthy.

Doubt about Father Persons had already begun to be felt in Rome and he was not rewarded for his efforts in the English College with a promotion to the office of Cardinal although a great deal was now expected of him. Without any titular authority, he was charged by the Cardinal-Protector of England to draw up a scheme of government for the rest of the clergy. His original idea was to establish a bishop in England and an archbishop in Flanders where there was a mirror of the problems in England. He used the fury of the persecution in England to drop the plan for a bishop. Some of the Seculars, led by Christopher Bagshawe, argued for the appointment of a bishop, but Father Persons disregarded their wishes and in England a hierarchy of priests was preferred. An Archpriest with assistants was appointed by the Cardinal-Protector. It is difficult to describe what an Archpriest is, but the position might be said to be somewhere between a Rural Dean and an Archdeacon. This was an entirely new form of ecclesiastical government and there was a great deal of feeling against it.

In March 1597, a Secular missioner priest, George Blackwell,[3] secretly living in and working from the house of Mrs Meany in Westminster, received a letter from Rome. The Cardinal-Protector, with the approval of Pope Clement VIII, was writing to inform him that he had appointed him Archpriest[4] over the Secular clergy in England. Six assistants were appointed for him and six were left to his discretion. He was to leave Mrs Meany's house and go to lodge at the town house of Anthony-Maria Browne, 2nd Viscount Montague, when he was in London. His instructions were that he was to work closely with Father Henry Garnet, the head of the Jesuit mission in England.

There is some dispute about how strongly the instruction was worded enjoining George Blackwell to work closely with the Jesuits. The version the Seculars appeared to believe Blackwell had received, and which they found so inflammatory, was that the Archpriest and his assistants were to determine nothing in any matter of importance without the Jesuits' consent. The Seculars saw the hand of Persons in this and it touched a nerve.

As well as the newly-appointed Archpriest, there was to be a new nuncio in Brussels, Frangipani, who had jurisdiction over the Archpriest. Even Frangipani believed that the arrangement in England gave excessive control to the Jesuits. In Europe, opinion was beginning to polarise as the vocal minority of English Secular priests began to make their anxieties heard. In the Spanish Netherlands, Richard Barret was given control of Secular priests there and was told to co-operate with Blackwell and to act against disruptive English priests.

It is clear that there was a very determined attempt to tie the hands of those Seculars who resented the Archpriest's imposition. The hard-won spirit of cooperation between Seculars and Regulars, which had been such an attractive feature of the settlement of the Wisbech Stirs, had evaporated. Father Henry Garnet, in constant contact with Father Persons, took charge of the Regulars.

George Blackwell, although a good scholar, with excellent qualifications on paper, and an amiable man, had none of the skills and experience necessary to calm the storm his appointment provoked. He had few successes and made many mistakes. He annoyed his clergy by the brusqueness of his manner and his preference for the opinions of the Jesuit Superior, Father Henry Garnet, over their own. The Seculars were affronted, fearful of their loss of independence, so that the split between Seculars and Regulars began to open again.

Another leading priest, Dr William Bishop, had joined the Appellants (as they were later to be known after signing the Appeal for a Bishop in 1600). It was he who, twenty years later, was to become the first Catholic Bishop of England (the Vicar Apostolic), since the Reformation. In 1598, the Secular priests chose Dr Bishop, with Robert Charnock, to travel to Rome to complain about the appointment of Blackwell. The alternative they were commissioned to seek was a Vicar Apostolic with full episcopal powers. They did this with 'the secret aid of Elizabeth's government'.[5] They were also to let it be known that they had considerable support for their grievance amongst the other Secular clergy. This first rather clumsy attempt in December 1598 to lay the Appellant case before the Holy See was ill fated. On their arrival Dr Bishop and Robert Charnock were arrested by the Cardinal-Protector. They were imprisoned at the English College for three months under Father Robert Persons.

On 6 April 1599, in Rome, the appointment of the Archpriest was confirmed in a Brief. Then the two Seculars, Bishop and Charnock, were released and dismissed from Rome. They were not allowed to return home as a sentence of exclusion from England was imposed and not lifted until further representations and another deputation to Rome four years later.

In England, following the failure of the Seculars' first attempt, a scholarly Jesuit, Thomas Lister,[6] was consulted as to what he thought about the conduct of those refusing obedience to the Archpriest and who had appealed to the Holy See. Pious and able, Lister was somewhat lacking in judgement. He wrote a treatise in which the perceived disobedience of the Seculars was violently censured. He declared them to have fallen into schism and irregularity and that they were deserving of excommunication. It is doubtful whether the tract was ever published but it was widely circulated in manuscript. It caused a great deal of resentment and fanned the flames of the heated dispute between the Seculars and the Regulars. Blackwell was supported by some of the Secular priests but others were outraged and asked the Archpriest to repudiate the tract. They were met with this curt response:

> Your request is that we should call in the treatise against your schism, and this is unreasonable, because the medicine ought not to be removed until the sore is thoroughly cured. If it grieve you, I am not grieved thereat.

Although the Brief had been accepted in England, George Blackwell made yet another unwise decision and insisted that the priests involved in the appeal against him should make reparation for their sin of schism. The members of the Secular group were amongst the most intellectually able in the country and were more than qualified to deal with the charge of schism, which they denied. They began to devise a formal appeal to Rome signed by thirty-three priests including the two Appellant martyrs, Cadwallador and Drurie.

> He [Roger Cadwallador] also signed the appeal of the 33 priests against the Archpriest Blackwell on 17 November 1600. (*The Knaresborough Manuscript*)

Lister's tract with its accusation of schism was to form the first of six grounds on which was based the 'Appeal of thirty-three clergymen' against George Blackwell's administration. The second appeal to the Pope, which Roger Cadwallador had signed in 1600, was heard in 1602 after the Appellants had referred the matter to the theologians of the Sorbonne where the decision was given in their favour.

This ruling signalled that the French were being drawn to the side of the Seculars. The 'printing war' began in earnest as Blackwell condemned the French decision and published a decree forbidding the publication of any defence of the Appellants' conduct and threatening to suspend anyone who disagreed with his decision.

Poor George Blackwell – his threats were ignored and the Briefs, Appeals and Tracts which were being published against him and in support of a Bishop brought the matter into the public arena in England. The printing of the Seculars' pamphlets was partly funded by the English government who took sides with the Appellants against the Jesuits who had been the object of their fear and hatred for years. The French, who shared some of the same concerns, joined the argument and also produced pamphlets which helped to add fuel to the fire.

The royal policy of helping the Appellants with their cause, particularly by printing pamphlets, was implemented by Richard Bancroft, Bishop of London. He set himself to help the Appellants in other ways and cultivated some individuals amongst them. William Watson,[7] a Secular priest, was one such who was in the forefront of the pamphlet war against the Jesuit position and came to the attention of Robert Persons who attempted to put the case for the Jesuits. Persons angrily wrote of Watson that he was 'so wrong shapen and of so bad and blinking an aspect that he looked nine ways at once'.

Watson responded by requesting that there should be an addition to the Latin liturgy which in English read 'from the machinations of Persons, free us, O Lord'. By September 1601, William Watson had become a resident at Fulham Palace under the protection of Richard Bancroft. The Bishop supported the Seculars in their wish to travel to Rome and see Clement VIII by giving permits to travel and providing contacts.

With the support of the French ambassador in Rome, the Appellants were able to gain a hearing for their third appeal. On 5 October 1602, a new brief was issued 'condemning the conduct of the archpriest, and justifying the appellants from the charges of schism and rebellion, which had been urged against them'.

The Brief limited the Regulars' jurisdiction over the Seculars. It forbade the Archpriest in future, for the sake of peace, to communicate either with the Superior of the Jesuits in England or with the General of the Society in Rome on the concern of his office. George Blackwell was commanded to supply the first three vacancies that should occur in the number of his assistants with priests selected from amongst the Appellants. He was ordered to transmit all appeals to the Cardinal-Protector. The Brief concluded by 'condemning the past, and prohibiting all future publications in any manner connected with the present controversy'. It was a measured response from Rome and helped to calm the Controversy and end 'the printing wars', but the bad feeling between the Regulars and the Seculars continued.

Notes

1   Belmont papers, Fragment from the *Knaresborough Manuscript* at Ushaw.
2   'Robert Persons', (Catholic Encyclopedia, online).
3   'George Blackwell', (Wikipedia).
4   'Archpriest Controversy', (Catholic Encyclopedia, online), 1–3.
5   'English Catholics-Publications in Printing Wars', (http://faculty.history/ .wisc.edu/sommerville), 2013, 7–8.
6   'Thomas Lister', (Catholic Encyclopedia, online).
7   *Ibid.*, 1.

CHAPTER 9

The Protestation of Allegiance

I T MUST BE OBSERVED HERE that Mr Cadwallador was one of those priests who with Dr William Bishop, after Bishop of Calcedon, Mr Colleton and other ancient and learned priests, to the number of thirteen of the Secular clergy, made a publick declaration or Profession of their Allegiance in the late Queen's reign which gave satisfaction to that princess and her Council as to the matters of subjection and obedience to their civil governors. This declaration I say, Mr Cadwallador had subscribed with the rest.[1]

The Papal Brief of 5 October 1602 had only achieved a small part of what the Appellants had hoped for. They had failed to secure Episcopal government in England, which was what they most wanted. Their 'friends' in the government felt more strongly about other prohibitions, which they had required but which were missing, and took the Papal Brief badly. The Appellants had failed to persuade the Pope to include in the Brief the demands of their government supporters which sought to restrain priests, whether Secular or Regular, from provoking the state by interfering in political affairs. Nor did they obtain their petition that all Catholics should report any designs of which they learnt against the Queen.

Disappointed at the tenor of the Brief, Elizabeth and her ministers replied by issuing a proclamation on 5 November 1602, exactly a month after the Papal Brief. The Proclamation was for the banishment or execution of all Catholic Missionaries, only offering mercy if the leading Secular priests were to publicly acknowledge their duty to the Queen. Led by Dr William Bishop, who drew up the famous loyal address of 31 January 1603, thirteen priests protested their allegiance to her. The thirteen are listed in Dodd's *Church History of England* as Dr William Bishop, John Colleton, John Mush, Robert Charnock, with Roger Cadwallador and Robert Drurie, Francis Barnaby, Anthony Champney, John Boseville, Richard Button, Anthony Hebourn, John Jackson and Oswald Needham.

In the Protestation of Allegiance they acknowledged the Queen as their lawful sovereign and repudiated the claim of the Pope to release them from their duty to her. They expressed their abhorrence at the forcible attempts already made to restore the Catholic religion and their determination to reveal any further conspiracies against the Government which should come to their knowledge. In return they pleaded their loyalty to the Queen and to the State in as much as they were ready to render to Caesar the things that are Caesar's, so they might be permitted to yield to the successor of Peter that obedience which Peter himself might have claimed under the commission of Christ, and so to distinguish between their several duties and obligations as to be ready on the one hand 'to spend their blood in defence of her Majesty', but on the other, 'rather to lose their lives than infringe the lawful authority of Christ's Catholic Church'. The printing of the Protestation of Allegiance was undertaken by one of the printing presses under the control of Richard Bancroft, at that time Bishop of London, which had during the time of the 'printing wars' been used to support the Appellants' case.

It was condemned by the Jesuits for its promise to reveal future conspiracies. The repudiation of the Pope's deposing power was condemned by the theological faculty of Louvain. That the Pope did not have the power to depose a reigning monarch was basic to the Appellants' belief as they thought that there was no way forward for toleration of Roman Catholicism without it. Those involved in producing the Protestation of Allegiance were motivated in part by a desire to save the English Mission which was being threatened by the Government to the point of extinction. No condemnation of the Protestation of Allegiance came from Rome.

In the hands of Dr William Bishop, who was a superb manager, it may also have been an attempt to buy time. The Papal Brief had been directed towards clarifying the role of the Archpriest and putting the control of the Roman Catholic Church in England back into the hands of the Seculars, and in particular into the hands of the Appellants who had not departed from their main motivation 'the desire for a Bishop'. It is possible to see the Papal Brief and the Protestation of Allegiance as two more steps in the long game towards the prize of a Bishop.

Twenty years later Dr Bishop, its author, was to become the first Vicar Apostolic of England in 1623 when the petitions of 1602 by the Appellants were at last granted. He was a good choice although he was only to hold the office for ten months until he died, during which time he organized a systematic form of ecclesiastical government which still exists today.

The Protestation was not thought by the State to go far enough and was judged to be intrinsically unsatisfactory. Elizabeth never saw the document because at the time it was being discussed she was seized with what proved to be her last illness.

Note

1   *Knaresborough Manuscript* (from papers kept at Belmont).

CHAPTER 10

The Death of Elizabeth

ROGER CADWALLADOR could not have known that, at the time he was involved in the preparation of the Protestation of Allegiance, the Queen, clearly depressed and unwell, entered the fugue-like state from which she was never to recover. For days before her death she lay on the floor in complete silence growing steadily weaker. Eventually her ladies-in-waiting put her to bed. Her counsellors gathered around her and soft music was played to soothe her. She is said to have responded to the enquiry of Robert Cecil, her closest advisor, that she wished James Stuart, the son of Mary Queen of Scots, to be her successor. It was clear that she was about to die and old Archbishop Whitgift was called to her bedside where he knelt beside her in prayer for hours, until she died 'as mildly as a lamb, easily like a ripe apple from the tree'.

History does not record whether Blessed Roger was in London, because of a general amnesty allowing his release, when her body was brought from Richmond Palace on the Thames by boat. If he had been in the City on that day, he would have been part of a huge multitude which sighed, wept and groaned in grief as the coffin passed by and he would have seen an unforgettable sight. The coffin was sealed and covered but, as was the custom with funerals of the great, there was a wax effigy of the Queen arranged on the coffin. The effigy of Elizabeth was sumptuously dressed in royal robes and in one hand she held the orb, in the other the sceptre and on her head was a crown. She was accompanied throughout by a host of black-clad courtiers all the way to Westminster Abbey. In

the Abbey she was carried to the north aisle to the Chapel of
Henry VII. At her request she was buried in the unmarked grave of
her half-sister, Mary I. This was what she had asked for and this
action and her epitaph were her last pious and humble gestures of
allegiance to her Roman Catholic subjects.

Regno consortes et urna, hic obdormimus Elizabetha et Maria
sorores, in spe resurrectionis.[1]

We sisters, sharers in reigning, in a burial place and in the hope of
the resurrection are here fallen asleep.

Note

1   A.N. Wilson, *The Elizabethans* (London: Hutchison, 2011), p. 365.

CHAPTER 11

Regime Changes and a Sea-Change

There was a great deal of work going on quietly behind the scenes on behalf of James Stuart, the King of Scotland, as Queen Elizabeth lay dying.

Robert Cecil,[1] later Lord Salisbury, had been in secret correspondence with James Stuart for some months as a new reign drew near. Cecil had inherited his father's great capacity for loyalty and hard work and, as the Queen's death grew closer, he began to transfer his attention and abilities to the Scottish King. His management of James Stuart's accession was masterly, and all the more so because the succession was not settled until the last hours before and just after the Queen died.[2] James Stuart was a foreigner and Scotland was a foreign power. The law of England prohibited a foreign prince from inheriting land in England.

James's closest rival was Arabella Stuart,[3] although her claim appears slight compared with his. Arabella, unlike James, had the advantage of being English and, to make matters doubly worse, from James Stuart's point of view, had an attachment to William Seymour, grandson of Lady Catherine Grey. Catherine Grey had been an heiress to the throne by the will of Henry VIII who had preferred the claims of his younger sister Mary to those of Margaret from whom James and Arabella Stuart descended. Much was made of Arabella's Catholic tendencies, which were probably non-existent, in order to bring her to London under guard while the way was prepared for James Stuart. Cecil had already received advice that Arabella was the focus of a plot against Cecil's preferred successor. Arabella was highly strung, unworldly and intellectual.

It was to prove unfortunate for her that she had fallen under the eye of the new king's chief asset, Robert Cecil. After promising not to, Arabella eloped and married Seymour and was captured and placed in prison where she went out of her mind and died.

Within a few hours of the death of Elizabeth, the first proclamation of the new king was made. Cecil had conjured up a text which he had prepared weeks before in his thorough and precise way. He read this proclamation with great pomp in three important locations in London and referred to James Stuart's 'undoubted' right to succeed. All this before the Queen had been dead for half a day. As night fell the first torch was thrust into the first bonfire and the signal was taken up by the lighting of previously prepared bonfires throughout the capital that the Queen was dead and a new king, James, had been declared. As the news of the Queen's death and news of her successor spread throughout the country bells were rung, trumpets sounded and local sheriffs processed carrying pictures of James I and VI and declaring that he was royally and rightly first in line from both houses of York and Lancaster.

In this triumph of organisation Catholics were placed in the forefront of these ostentatious celebrations. They provided barrels of wine for public feasts and threw money to the crowds and were generally involved in fuelling the jollity. Sir Thomas Tresham, the father of Francis Tresham, the infamous Gunpowder Plotter, was joyfully proclaiming King James in Northampton a day after the death of Elizabeth. Of all Catholic leaders he was perhaps the most senior and, in fairness, he had suffered fines and imprisonment under Elizabeth, but his response was typical of the whole Roman Catholic community. The Jesuits were anxious to be identified with these acts of patriotism and Father Henry Garnet wrote a letter which he hoped would find its way into the king's hands declaring that the Jesuits were dear and not unnatural subjects of the crown. James, after all, was the son of Mary Queen of Scots, the 'peerless martyr'.

There was a naïve hope both at home and abroad that James Stuart would convert to Roman Catholicism. Perhaps the most prominent amongst the foreign royalty who were said to share this baseless hope were the great Catholic Hapsburg Regent Archduke Albert and the Archduchess Isabella.

King James was never likely to become a Roman Catholic but he was a consummate politician and at the beginning of his reign was clever enough to present himself as the only child of the beautiful, doomed Mary Queen of Scots and the charming scallywag Henry Lord Darnley. Through his actions and own later writings it is clear that he opposed Roman Catholicism. The shadow of his unhappy and violent Scottish childhood under the watchful eyes of his harsh Calvinist mentors can be seen in what he wrote. What Roman Catholics believed, in his words, was satanic and demonic. His stress on fornication by her priests and idleness amongst monastics and the 'drooling' over Our Lady might also suggest that he had never come to terms with his fractured relationship with his Catholic mother. Because he would have seen the Pope as a rival prince, he saved the worst of his invective for the Holy Father, and is said to have declared that Rome was the 'Seat of the Antichrist'.

Ann of Denmark,[4] the wife of James Stuart, appears to have flirted with Roman Catholicism but her position was never clear nor would her husband, with his talent for prevarication, have allowed it to be. The papacy was never certain of her conversion and in 1612 Pope Paul V advised a nuncio, 'Not considering the inconsistancy of that Queen and the many changes she had made in religious matters and that even if it might be true that she might be a Catholic, one should not take on oneself any judgement'.

News of his accession had reached James at Holyrood Palace in Edinburgh within three days of Elizabeth's death. Robert Carey, a descendent of the Boleyn family, had ridden with breakneck speed to bring him the news. He knelt before James and greeted him as the King of England, Ireland, Scotland and France, since the Tudors had never renounced their title to the French throne.

Almost immediately James Stuart set off for London to secure the throne and every step of the way in England he was greeted by large crowds of friendly people who lavishly entertained both him and the party of Scottish nobles who accompanied him. He left behind the poverty of Scotland which he described as a 'stony couch' for England which he saw as a 'featherbed', and he got the impression that England was a wealthy country – a sort of money tree which was ripe and ready for shaking. In the forefront of this display of riches, apparently offering themselves to him, were his Roman Catholic subjects.

He made the journey from Scotland so quickly that he had to wait outside London while the old Queen was buried, a ceremony which was carried out reverently and, as tradition dictated, one month after her death.

As the successor to the Tudor dynasty, James Stuart must have appeared to be almost perfect in comparison with any other candidate. He was thirty-six, young enough to be active and interesting and perhaps amenable to influence, but old enough to have gained some wisdom. He had experience of the art of kingship almost from birth. He could trace his bloodline back to Henry VII. He was male and had an apparently stable marriage and there was a 'royal family'. His wife, Ann of Denmark, who was a princess in her own right, had borne him five children already, three of them surviving. Of those three, two of them were male and the eldest, Henry (what better name!), was healthy and attractive. It is not surprising that the people of England were happy to put the dark days of fear and instability and barrenness behind them and start to look forward in hope to better days.

Robert Cecil, First Minister of James I, was a vital link between the Elizabethan and Stuart governments. He was the second son of William Cecil, Elizabeth's great minister, Lord Burghley, and a year after the death of the father in 1598, the son succeeded him as Master of the Wards. A staunch Protestant, he was frail and unprepossessing in appearance, being very short and with a twisted back. James Stuart may have been in correspondence with Cecil since before 1601 but when they first met in 1603 James, who owed him his smooth accession, mocked his physical appearance. 'Though you are but a little man, we will shortly load your shoulders with business', and later called him his, 'little beagle'. No one, other than the king, would have taken the risk of mocking Cecil to his face as he cleverly made himself indispensable.

Lord Salisbury, as he became in 1605, worked tirelessly to fulfil his royal master's expectations but if he had lost office he had a 'fall-back' plan. He was described by others close to the throne as 'a devouring flame'. He had busily secured his own position before Elizabeth died by throwing himself into land speculation. He had spent £30,000 on buying land and property in 1602 as well as borrowing heavily from London Aldermen. While the new king idled the time away talking and hunting with his royal favourites or spent the money which Cecil raised for him, his loyal servant had his watchful eye on every corner of the kingdom and he appears to have missed nothing and was able to put his own spin on everything.

The death of Bishop Herbert Westfaling of Hereford in 1602 necessitated the appointment of a new Bishop. The man chosen for the diocese and the first of the Jacobean bishops was Robert Bennet.[5] He had had a relatively successful career at Cambridge University where he was noted for his erudition and where he distinguished himself on the tennis court. He was known at Cambridge for his good looks which were later to do him no harm with James I who is reported to have said of Robert Bennet that 'if he were to chuse a Bishop by the aspect, he would chuse him of all the men he had seen, for a grave reverent and pleasing countenance'.

Robert Bennet became master of the hospital of St Cross in Winchester in 1583 where he helped to eradicate Catholic recusancy. This made him enemies but also brought him to the favourable attention of the father of Robert Cecil, William Lord Burghley, who gave him this senior Church position which had become vacant. When he was unsuccessful in gaining later preferment he complained to William Cecil that he was unwilling to be buried 'amongst beggers'. 'Beggers' was what he called the bedesmen of the hospital which was in his care.

Bennet felt very strongly about his own propriety in death. He left £500, a huge sum in those days, for his burial expenses. He also selected a preacher for the service and designed his own sumptuous monument. Bishop Bennet's tomb is in the north aisle of Hereford Cathedral, behind the place in the choir where his wife used to sit. Only the base and the effigy remain of a once much more impressive edifice. He specified how much cloth was to be used and the price for the cloak of each person who participated. He designed a very different death for Roger Cadwallador.

Robert Bennet appears to have been a man who had a high opinion of himself and was not pleased to be passed over for promotion, complaining to Cecil that a number of his own pupils had been 'advaunced to the highest callinges in this church'.

Sir William Cecil, Lord Burghley, took the point and in 1596 Robert Bennet was promoted and became Dean of Windsor as well as continuing as master of St Cross. He received other appointments which brought him to the attention of the court. It was not all plain sailing and he spent a short time in prison for objecting to the Queen's proposed marriage to a French Catholic prince but he would not have displeased Cecil by his objection and was soon released. Later he upset the Queen again because he was unable to transfer a lease belonging to the hospital of St Cross. To his disgust he had to turn down the Bishopric of Salisbury because the promotion was dependent on his transferring leases to the crown which he was unable to do. This time he railed in such a derogatory way at the man who was made Bishop of Salisbury that Robert Cecil who, like his father, preferred the subtle approach, rebuked him for his 'medling'.

Unabashed, Bennet continued to seek promotion and soon succeeded by preaching a well-received sermon to the court. In January 1603, as the old Queen lay dying, he was installed as Bishop of Hereford. He was the archetypal 'new broom' ignoring the opinions of traditionalists in the Close, particularly that of the popular dean, Charles Langford, whom the diocese had requested by petition to be their Bishop. Langford was particularly interested in the cathedral school and endowed some exhibitions for boys from Hereford. His contribution was not acknowledged and when he died in 1607 he was buried in the cathedral church without any memorial.

Bishop Bennet does not appear to have been happy in Hereford and found the diocese 'pestered with recusants, they persist in bold contempt of all that I do'. Lord Salisbury had put him there in part to deal with the problem of recusancy. It is also possible that he may have been placed in Hereford to keep an eye on the considerable Cecil interests in the Marches where the Cecils owned a great deal of land.

Robert Bennet was very much a member of the Reformed wing of the Church of England. In his later episcopacy, and after the execution of Roger Cadwallador, he was unable to gain his sought-for promotion out of the Diocese and became prominent in sponsoring evangelical activity. He was instrumental in setting up a combination lecture at Leintwardine in 1612. He dealt with low clerical standards by ousting absentee ministers and presiding over diocesan visitations. He embarked on a diocesan training programme for non-preaching ministers and worked with non-conformists such as the Puritans.

It is not possible to know if Blessed Roger[6] was released from prison under a general amnesty at the time of the new King's accession, but everything that follows suggests that he returned to the Marches about this time and did not leave again. He is known to have been in Herefordshire in 1603 because Bishop Bennet accused him of being involved in the Bye Plot.

Soon after the King's accession there was a Mass held in the heart of Hereford at Candlemass with more than 140 people present, perhaps signalling hope for toleration during the new reign and, possibly, the welcome return of a popular parish priest.

There appears to have been a profound change in Roger's thinking as the prospect of a Bishop responsible for England and a political solution bringing about a change in the approach to Catholic toleration appeared to be more likely. Basing himself in the Marches he prepared to attend to the more pressing needs of his parishioners. He maintained his loyalty to the 'English party' while the prickly relationship with the Jesuits in the county appears to have continued until they did him a great service on the day of his execution.

After his return to Herefordshire he was described in the words of Bishop Bennet as 'Cadwallador the priest in these parts'.

Notes

1   'Robert Cecil', *Oxford Dictionary of National Biography, Vol. 10* (Oxford: Oxford University Press, 2004), pp. 746–759.
2   A. Frazer, *The Gunpowder Plot* (St Ives: Orion, 2002), pp. xx-xxv.
3   R.K. Marshall, 'Arabella Stuart', *Oxford Dictionary of National Biography, Vol. 53* (Oxford: Oxford University Press, 2004), pp. 132–133.
4   'Ann of Denmark', (Wikipedia), 1–7.
5   'Robert Bennet', *Oxford Dictionary of National Biography, Vol. 15* (Oxford: Oxford University Press), pp. 112–113.
6   B. Rees, 'Roger Cadwallador', *Oxford Dictionary of National Biography, Vol. 9* (Oxford: Oxford University Press, 2004), pp. 424–425.

CHAPTER 12

The Bye Plot

THE BYE PLOT[1] occurred soon after the accession of James I. It was called 'Bye' in the sense of 'by the way' because it was far less serious in its aims than the principal or 'Main' plot. The aim of the Main Plot was to replace James I with Arabella Stuart and happened at the same time as the Bye Plot. Another name for the Bye Plot was the 'Surprising Treason'.

Two years after the Bye Plot there was an attempt by Bishop Robert Bennet, on 22 June 1605, to link Roger Cadwallador with the conspiracy in order to obtain a Commission from Lord Salisbury. In a letter to the Earl of Salisbury, Bishop Bennet wrote:

> It is also insinuated that Cadwallador the priest and William Morgan were actors and had their finger in the intended treason, which was in part hammered in these parts.[2]

The Bye Plot had been devised by William Watson,[3] the Appellant. It was he who had lived for a time in the household of the Bishop of London. He had hurried up to Scotland when the Queen died to offer James I the loyalty of his party. In return for this it was hoped, not without cause, that the King would show religious toleration to Catholics and cease to exact fines on recusants. This was not a groundless hope. There were copies of letters circulating in the Marches containing promises of toleration of Roman Catholicism by James I as he made his way down through the country to London in 1603. These were referred to in a letter which was eventually delivered into the hands of the Lord Bishop of Hereford who did not depart from his hard-line stance deploring the promises which, 'therby gave them [recusants] encouragement & hope of tolleracon'.

James I saw himself as needing more money not less, having not one household to maintain, as in the case of Queen Elizabeth, but five. That is one for himself, his wife and each of his three children as well as funding an extravagant lifestyle for them and the Scots who had accompanied him to England. There was to be no diminution of the fines on recusants but the King, who was very good at enigmatic and acceptable answers, gave the strong impression that there might be.

Watson came back to London full of hope but very soon, when the longed-for toleration of recusants was not forthcoming, he was bitterly disappointed. He gathered a group of men around him who also wished for religious toleration for their respective denominations. With another priest, William Clark, and a number of laymen, including a Puritan, Thomas Grey, 15th Baron Grey de Wilton, and a Protestant courtier, George Brooke, he talked excitably about taking King James prisoner. This was to be done by seizing and imprisoning him, a method which had its precedent in Scotland. The plotters would capture the Tower of London where William Watson would be promoted to Lord Keeper and convert the imprisoned King James to Catholicism. It all sounds very idealistic and unlikely and some of the conspirators thought better of it and soon withdrew. The others persisted but, not surprisingly, it was a complete failure.

Father Henry Garnet, the Jesuit Prefect, George Blackwell, the Archpriest, and John Gerard, a Jesuit, betrayed the plot to the authorities. Bishop Richard Bancroft of London had washed his hands of his earlier friendship with Watson who was now a hunted man. He fled westward, perhaps in an attempt to leave the country for Ireland.

It might have been that at this point that Roger Cadwallador entered the story, as Watson would have been desperate for help. Roger would have been aware, from letters in circulation, that Watson had been given good reason for hope of religious toleration, however mistaken his method in trying to achieve this end. It may have been that he responded to pleas from the virtually blind Watson for help and provided him with a guide to lead him safely out of the county. The guide let Watson down by disappearing into an alehouse for a drink, leaving the priest, vulnerable because of his poor eyesight, outside where he was captured by Bishop Bennet's men. Local legend puts the site of the arrest in a field outside Hay-on-Wye but it may have been in Abergavenny. This was close enough to Cadwallador territory to implicate Roger in the eyes of the Bishop, but there was never any question of arresting him at the time and it was not until two years later, in 1605, that Bennet suggested that Roger had 'a finger in the plot'. 1605 was the year of 'the Commotion at Allensmore'. This was also a year in which paranoia, suspicion, and sanctions against Roman Catholics were increasing, and led to despair and distrust, and the Gunpowder Plot.

The Main and the Bye plotters were tried together. The two Bye Plot priests, Watson and Clark, were executed as was the Protestant George Brooke, while the other conspirators were reprieved.

Notes

1   'Bye Plot', (Wikipedia).
2   State Papers, 14, Vol. XIV, 52.
3   N.W.S. Cranfield, 'William Watson' (*Oxford Dictionary of National Biography*, online).

CHAPTER 13

The Commotion at Allensmore

IN 1605 AN EVENT OCCURRED IN Herefordshire in the small village of Allensmore relating to the death and illegal burial of Alice Wellington, the wife of a yeoman. It became known as the 'Allensmore Commotion' and was to rock the country.

Allensmore lay deep in Roger Cadwallador country and Alice Wellington was one of his parishioners and was, in some versions of the story, a convert to Catholicism or, as the Diocesan Histories[1] puts it, she had been 'seduced to Romanism'. She was to die firm in recusancy and excommunicated from the Church of England and so was excluded from burial in consecrated ground in the church-yard. Later apologias suggest that it is false to say that she was refused burial but her family and her Catholic neighbours strongly believed that that was what 'excommunicate' meant. A gentleman in London quoted in the Diocesan Histories and writing at the time plainly states: 'she [Alice] died excommunicate, and, as the vicar refused to bury her, the Papists undertook this office'.

Alice Wellington was described in a contemporary pamphlet as 'a simple woman, and voyd of any true grounds of Learning or Divinity'. Another dismissive description of a Catholic convert who was the wife of a yeoman, which betrays an attitude to her faith which saw only superstition and ignorance at the heart of her beliefs. Thomas Wellington was a man of substance and deeply committed to his religion. He and his wife had refused to send their children for Anglican baptism and the church court rolls record that they paid for this decision.

Allensmore,[2] originally named 'Alan's-moor', is built on

marshland reclaimed in the thirteenth century. It is a little more than three and a half miles southwest of Hereford. It is easy to pass by, but turn left from the A456 and follow the winding lanes which lead eventually to the hamlet with its church of St Richard.

Even today there are almost no stones from which the square-towered church was built which were not placed there by Roman Catholic hands. There can be no doubt that the exclusion of Catholics caused resentment and the wounds of the Reformation would still have been very raw at the time of the 'Commotion'. The church building would have been well known to Blessed Roger's parishioners and some of them would have had close family buried in the churchyard. The Vicarage is close to the church and was the home at that time of Richard Heyns who had had to admit at a Visitation in 1605 that no sermon had been preached since Christmastide and not many before that. It appears that he was not popular with his parishioners and had fences to mend with his fellow Anglican clergy.

There are several attractive half-timbered houses in the parish which may have been known to Roger Cadwallador but most of his Allensmore parishioners at the time of the Commotion would have been described by Bishop Challoner as 'of the poorer sort'. Some of the people of Allensmore were extremely poor. Their homes were wretched huts constructed of clay and sods and branches. These mud huts were primitive, small and crammed together on the verges of the winding lanes. Some of the inhabitants grew vegetables and a few kept chickens or a pig, but these were limited in number. They were a community that was numbered in hundreds. Their main occupation was spinning flax and hemp. Both were woven into cloth, and hemp made strong ropes for horse halters and for shipping purposes as well as for the hangman. Unfortunately for many of these destitute people it was almost impossible to find the few shillings to buy a bale with which to work. They were forced to beg or steal from the orchards and gardens or glean the fields. Sometimes as many as three hundred were seen gleaning a single field. The right to glean was very ancient but their numbers, dire poverty and their Catholic religion may have made them objects of suspicion and even fear by some of their more well-off neighbours.

It is thought that Blessed Roger stepped out of the shadows in May 1605 to go to the bedside of his dying parishioner, Alice Wellington. In Herefordshire May is one of the most beautiful months. The green of the hedgerows and trees is fragile and fresh, and blossom is everywhere. It was the priest's practice to walk, and no doubt as he passed the mud hut village the people would have recognised him and been aware of his reason for being there but would have been circumspect in their greetings and watchful of strangers in order to keep him safe.

Professor Duffy's book, *The Stripping of the Altars*, has been the major source of information for what may have occurred next at the deathbed of Alice Wellington. Priests of that time were skilled in the 'Art of Death'. Texts show that the presence of a priest at the bedside of the dying was to give comfort and the reassurance of salvation, although the reality of evil and the perils of Hell were not shirked any more than the sinfulness of the dying parishioner. The constant emphasis was on the power and will of God to save and the all-sufficient merits of the crucified Christ who required nothing but repentance and faith to give salvation to the dying.

As he entered the room of the dying woman, in a single gesture which was designed to be both Christocentric and compassionate, Roger Cadwallador would have held up a crucifix before her eyes. Then with quiet comforting words he would have exhorted the dying Alice to focus only on her Saviour, 'Put alle thi trust in his passion and in his deth, and thenke thereon, and non-other thing. With his deth medil thee and wrap thee ... and have the crosse to fore thee'.

After giving gentle reassurance, some questions would follow. These were to discover whether or not she rejected heresy and wished to die in the Faith of the Church. He would have asked her if she recognised and repented her sins and put all her trust in Christ's passion and not in any merits of her own.

His next duty was to make sure that she was in charity with her neighbours. She was to forgive any who had wronged her and, as far as possible, she was to try to make reparation to any whom she had wronged. After this deathbed scrutiny and being sure of her penitence, Blessed Roger would have absolved her and anointed her and she would have received the Blessed Sacrament.

It was believed that in these last vulnerable moments the Devil was at his most active and would attempt to slip in and pluck her from the arms of God. The priest's role was to help her to die well by making sure that she did not slip into heresy, superstition, infidelity or despair. He was to prevent her from sinning against charity by refusing to accept her situation which was God-given and to stop her abusing those who tended her deathbed. He was there to prevent her from forfeiting salvation by trusting in her own good deeds rather than solely in Christ. He would do what he could to prevent her from rejecting Heaven and the eternal world by clinging to the goods and relationships of the present one. Roger and her relatives and friends stood between the Devil and Alice Wellington and would do so until her burial.

In this fight against the Devil the bedroom became a crowded battlefield. Alice and her family would have been supported by the bonds of simple neighbourliness which would find religious expression. Sprinkling with holy water was mandatory. This practice was abhorred by the Protestant hierarchy whose real concern was to condemn anyone who used this ceremony to bring blessing in the traditional way. The lay person in Allensmore with a reputation for sanctity and who knew the right prayers would have been called to the deathbed in order to help her to make a good death and would have stayed to the end.

Death involved the whole community, on earth and in heaven. Above all, Mary the Mother of Christ was the saint of the deathbed. She was always on the side of the sinner and in his or her favour would tilt the scales held by St Michael the Archangel. St Michael was the other great saint of the deathbed because it was he who stood at the door between this world and the next.

The crowded bedchamber had another more practical side, since it was now that Alice Wellington would have made her will so that in this way, as well as being reconciled to God, she could be reconciled to her neighbours. At this time Alice would have bequeathed her most cherished possessions and spoken of her loving wish to order lasting relationships among her friends and family after her death. At that moment of leaving the world she would have wanted to prolong her memory within the community of the living by bequests and requests for regular prayers of intercession in order to reduce the time she would spend in Purgatory. All of this was outlawed and Anglican clergy were to dissuade the dying from providing in their wills for traditional works and instead to place money in the poor box so that there could be no provision for the 'cult' of the Blessed Sacrament or that of the dead.

Alice probably died very early in the morning of Tuesday 21 May 1605 in the week after Pentecost. It was the practice amongst Papists at that time for burial to follow almost immediately after death. First the body would have been wrapped in a shroud and placed in a coffin and, following usual practice, a Requiem Mass celebrated. It may be that at this point gravediggers were dispatched to the churchyard to dig her grave.

There is some disagreement about those present but the main characters are not disputed. The numbers present vary in some accounts between twenty-five and sixty but it is generally agreed that there were enough people to constitute a crowd.[3]

At about five o'clock, just after sunrise, a large crowd of relatives and friends is said to have brought Alice's body to the churchyard at Allensmore for burial in consecrated ground. Richard Heyns, the Vicar of Allensmore, said that he was woken early by the ringing of a little bell and he went to the window of his Vicarage, which adjoined the churchyard, to see where the sound was coming from.

The bell signalled the start of the prayers of intercession and the seven penitential psalms. It was being rung by a weaver from the village, Richard Smith, whom he recognised. He was part of a funeral party of about fifty people who processed in the traditional way behind the cross which was carried around the churchyard following the 'course' of the sun. Heyns had recognised the crucifer at once as Philip Giles of Winnall. He knew Phillip Giles because he was a man of some standing in the county. Others he could identify were William Chadnor and another weaver, William Marsh of Kingstone, and William Caunt of Madley. 'There was no one else of any standing that I know of', he was to tell the Bishop.

Several people had 'tapers burning and other trumperies' by which he may have meant rosaries or pictures of the saints or homemade crosses, all of which were highly illegal. These people went ahead of the coffin leading the procession. Processions had been proscribed since 1547. This was on the pretext of eliminating 'all contention and strife' as a procession might become a riotous or violent assembly and there were to be no more 'in church or other place'. Richard Heyns would have considered this display superstitious and indecent and distracting from 'the Word'.

Mr Heyns later reported that some of the party were armed with swords and staves and clustered together. Perhaps this was to hide the cassocked figure of a priest. Close to the priest was James Coles, excommunicated the November before, who was known to be the 'Massing clerk' to Roger Cadwallador. There were several women in the funeral procession as well. The only ones Mr Heyns recognised were Joan, possibly the daughter of the deceased Alice Wellington, and Alice Coles, who was married to James Coles who was a weaver as well as being Roger Cadwallador's clerk.

The outraged vicar hurried to get dressed. He did not see Alice Wellington's shrouded body reverently removed from the coffin and gently laid to rest among her family who had gone to the grave before her. He did not see the cassocked priest turn to the body and speak directly to her in Latin, 'I commend thy soul to God the Father Almighty, and thy body to the ground, earth to earth, ashes to ashes, dust to dust'. In the new prayer book liturgy the living rather than dead were addressed. As he spoke the priest scattered earth on her and then the gravediggers filled in the grave.

The mourners could go no further with her and having done everything that they could they turned away from the grave to be faced with the figure of the Vicar who was incandescent with rage. He remonstrated with them and they responded most insultingly, perhaps jostling and distracting him while the priest escaped. After that Mr Heyns set off to the Bishop's Palace to tell his Lordship what he had seen. Those he was able to name out of the dozens he said were at the burial were very limited. In a letter to Lord Salisbury on 22 June 1605, Bishop Bennet says that Roger Cadwallador said Mass at Whitfield, the home of Sir Charles Morgan later that day, which placed him in the area of Allensmore.

Robert Bennet took three days to plan what he was going to do next, possibly so that he could make the best use of the situation to bring about the capture of Roger Cadwallador. The Bishop issued an arrest warrant for those that Richard Heyns had recognised but included an extra name, Leonard Marsh, who had not been named by Heyns but whom it would appear the Bishop wanted to interrogate.

Three days after the burial of Alice Wellington, the High Constable of the Hundred, George Wenlond, assisted by a group of ten or a dozen men, arrived in the village of Hungerstone. Hungerstone is close to Allensmore and it was where James Coles and William Chadnor worked as weavers in adjoining rooms. Both of these men had been named by Richard Heyns as being present at the illegal burial. This is the likely reason that the High Constable had started the arrests at the Coles' home in Hungerstone.

James Coles would have been privy to a great deal of information about the priest and later evidence suggests that the Bishop would have had no scruples about attempting to force it from him. James was in a very vulnerable position, as capture might result in torture and violent death because lay Catholics were at risk as well as their priests. A Yorkshire martyr, Blessed Margaret Clitheroe, had suffered and died terribly for harbouring a priest, John Mush, who was a fellow Appellant and co-signatory of the Protestation of Allegiance with Blessed Roger. James Coles would have known of this and may possibly have made up his mind already that he would do what he could to avoid capture. It appears that his fellow Catholics had resolved to protect their priest and help his 'Massing clerk' and anyone of their number who was captured and might be tortured for information.

The two weavers were surprised and seized but William Chadnor escaped and some of the posse pursued him. James Coles was probably more closely guarded than Chadnor, but while his guards were distracted he picked up a short knife, used in his trade, and cut one of them on the chin and another in several places on his hand. Then Leonard Marsh came in and helped James Coles to escape, but was captured himself and led off to Hereford. This prisoner appears to have been very significant to the High Constable who enlisted some passers-by to assist them to convey Leonard Marsh to Hereford, and the number of men increased to sixteen.

Because of the humiliation of what happened next the High Constable was at pains to stress that they were very lightly armed. They made a little progress towards Hereford with their prisoner until they reached the ridge close to where Belmont Abbey now stands. The posse was halted here by William Marsh, Leonard's brother, and asked to wait until William Morgan of Treville Park should arrive and have a word with them. The High Constable appears to have wished to avoid having a conversation with one of the leading Catholic supporters of the priest in the county and pushed on to Hereford, with the prisoner resisting all the way.

Very soon the posse was met with a force of forty or fifty men armed with bows and arrows, staves, bill hooks and swords, and George Wenlond was ordered to release the prisoner or 'see his own guts spilt'. The rescuers had added another Gentleman to their number, John Philipps of Kivernoll, and this was noted by Wenlond. Wisely the High Constable agreed to release the prisoner and then set off back to Hereford empty-handed but unharmed. He had noticed several other people he recognised among Leonard Marsh's rescuers. When he arrived in Hereford he gave this information to the Bishop who appears to have been determined to make as much political capital as he could out of the situation and dispatched the news of 'the riot' to the Privy Council in London.

The Privy Council sent Sir Herbert Croft, of Croft Castle near Shobdon, to serve on the Council for the Marches following the Commotion at Allensmore. There seems be no doubt that he was a staunch Anglican at the time and was responsible for dismissing some of the Justices of the Peace who were suspected of having recusant leanings. It may be that he did not accept the Bishop's heated version of events because his name was dropped from the record. He was later to be received into the Roman Catholic faith and, for the last five years of his life, he was a Benedictine monastic in the community at Douai.

In the Diocesan Histories of Hereford, it is reported that some of those involved were captured and sent to London to answer for their conduct. Later, the Earl of Worcester came to Raglan and is said to have reasoned so strongly with the offenders that they forsook their Papist ways and became Protestants. John Griffiths was one of these. Records compiled by the Bishop of Hereford and the Earl of Worcester[4] show that it cost those who were captured a great deal. There are five listed in the court records including Leonard and William Marsh. All five confessed and four of them were incarcerated for three months and fined the equivalent in today's money of £1,000. One of the five took the Oath of Submission and was dismissed.

Bishop Bennet blamed the earlier perceived lack of firmness and the spreading of 'false' rumours of the king's desire for toleration for encouraging Papists to rebellion. The King made a three-hour-long speech to the robed judges at the Court of Greenwich on Sunday June 9th in which he made it plain that there was no need to spare the blood of recusants and that the Catholics of Herefordshire should serve as an example. State papers record that the number of recusants continued to grow in the Marches at this time.

The Bishop was also keen to point out, to anyone who would

listen, that recusants from Lancashire, Yorkshire, Oxfordshire, Berkshire, Gloucestershire, Warwickshire, Somerset and Dorset were moving into the county in large numbers. They congregated around the Cwm, Llanrothal and the Darrow and were served by Jesuit priests. The concern of the Bishop was that recusants of the Jesuit persuasion were more likely to take up arms against the King and had assistance from foreign powers. However much the Bishop tried to sow seeds of dissension, there is no evidence that the Jesuits and their supporters were involved in the Commotion at Allensmore, and if there was trouble afterwards this was caused by the laity's need to defend themselves and their priests.

On 19 June Sir James Scudamore of Holme Lacey, who had become M.P. for Herefordshire in 1604, with three other Justices, and supported by heavily armed men, made a thirty-mile sweep of the Herefordshire Marches. Village by village, house by house, all that night and all of the following day they made a meticulous search. They found 'altars, images, books of superstition, relics of idolatry' but hardly a living soul apart from a few children and elderly women. The villages were deserted. The entire population appeared to have fled westwards and southwards. The 'Commotion' died down as quickly as it had arisen.

Roger Cadwallador is said to have taken refuge with the Berringtons at Winsley House at Hope under Dinmore.[5]

Notes

1   H.W. Phillott, *Diocesan Histories, Hereford* (Hereford: SPCK, 1888), pp. 194–196.

2   M.A. Raven, *A Guide to Herefordshire* (Hereford: Michael Raven, 1996), p. 10.

3   R. Matthias, *Whitsun Riot* (London: Bowes & Bowes, 1963), pp. 2–3.

4   J. Matthews, *Records Relating to Catholicism in South Wales Marches, 17th and 18th centuries*, Catholic Record Society, Miscellanea II (London, 1906), pp. 289–297.

5   N.C. Reeves, *The Parish of St Ethelbert, Leominster* (Leominster: Norman C. Reeves, 1972), pp. 33–34.

CHAPTER 14

Taken!

THERE DOES NOT APPEAR to be any record to tell us whether it was an act of betrayal or foolishness which delivered Roger Cadwallador into the hands of Bishop Robert Bennet. The information from the Belmont archives[1] says that he was apprehended on Easter Day, 11 April 1610, at the house of Mrs Winifred Scroope, a widow, who lived in the area of Weston Beggard, within eight miles of Hereford, although some records put the arrest at Stretton Court.

Weston Beggard, even today, is an area of undulations and hedges, and the Under-Sheriff's party of armed men could hide quite easily while biding their time until their quarry could be seized. The archive says that it was James Prychard, the Under-Sheriff of the county of Herefordshire, who arrested him, and he also took away with him some 'church stuffe'.

At the time, 'church stuffe' may have included some articles similar to those that can be seen at the Stonyhurst College museum today where they keep a pony-skin bag which was carried by a priest like Blessed Roger, and which contained many of the things that were needed for saying Mass. It includes a chasuble sewn together using the brocade from a woman's gown, and a stole, maniple and corporal veil from the same dress. Many Catholic homes in those times would have cherished an altar stone which may have been an oblong piece of slate, probably not more than two feet by one foot, which could have been pushed into a fireplace or a wall in order to hide it. There may have been a chalice (this would have been very small as only the priest would have communicated in both kinds) and a paten which, like the chalice, could be easily hidden amongst household cups and plates in the same way as purificators and altar linen could have been secreted amongst the household laundry if the Mass was interrupted. If they had been found, any one of these articles would have been highly incriminating.

On that Easter Day the prisoner was brought to the High Sheriff's dwelling where he was kept until the following afternoon. He would have spent the night in the unwholesome depths of a prison cell shackled to the wall and heavily guarded. His was a 'mind alive' and he would have spent those miserable hours of his imprisonment collecting his thoughts and planning a strategy for what lay ahead, which he knew would be a 'battayle', possibly the final battle with Bishop Bennet whose hated quarry he had been for seven years. He would have been aware that there could be no honourable return to freedom after the next day's encounter. A letter written by Roger shortly after his capture makes it clear that he was aware that the Oath of 1606 was the issue and that he would be offered the alternative of 'doubtful promises': if he would 'conforme or swear' and, if he would not, then the consequence would be the 'Sword of Death' or at best 'imprisonment or banyshment'.

To have any chance of freedom he would have had to take the Oath of Allegiance to King James I.[2] This was a very different document from the Protestation of Allegiance of 1603 which had been drawn up by William Bishop and the twelve other Appellants, including the two martyrs, Drurie and Cadwallador. The Protestation of Allegiance had not been condemned by Rome, unlike the Oath of 1606 which had been condemned by the Pope who said, 'It cannot be taken as it contains many things evidently contrary to faith and salvation'. It had at its heart a rejection of the 'Divine Right of Kings'. In many ways the Act was ambiguous but it contained the phrase that anyone who refused it was 'impious, heretical and damnable' which meant that it was a betrayal of other Catholics who dissented from the Oath. King James said in 1606 it was 'an Act for the better discovering and repressing of Popish recusants'.

George Blackwell, the Archpriest, after initial hesitation, first refusing, then allowing, then refusing, finally accepted the Oath while in prison. He had been kept under the close personal supervision of the King. The King undertook to answer the missives sent to Blackwell from Rome. At first the replies to the King, which came from Cardinal-Protector Bellarmine, SJ,[3] were also anonymous. Later the King went into print and his arguments were printed as a tract using his own name which was answered, also as a printed tract, by the Cardinal, who now used his own name. St Robert Bellarmine's involvement shows that the debate was no longer a point of principle only for English Catholics because it had drawn in figures from much of Western Europe. It raised the profile of both protagonists, King James in his defence of Calvinist Protestantism, and Bellarmine because of his defence of Tridentine Catholicism.[4]

Unfortunately Blackwell accepted the Oath, on the grounds of the King's reassurance that no encroachment on conscience was intended. It is sad to read that he had some success in encouraging the faithful to apostasy. With the King's keen support, he continued to defend his position for two years before he was eventually suspended and a new Archpriest, George Birkett, was appointed in 1608.

Loyal Catholics would argue that the Oath amounted to a statement beforehand of 'the conditions under which the Holy See will be disobeyed'. Rome has always considered this position dishonourable in the same way as a nation would consider it a disgrace to lay down the terms under which her soldiers were to desert or capitulate. This was the 'poison in the sequel' of which Blessed Roger was to speak on the scaffold.

The Appellant John Mush, also a signatory to the Protestation of Allegiance 1603, and who had been the confessor to Margaret Clitheroe, became the new Archpriest Birkett's secretary. This group of whom Bishop, Mush, Drurie and Cadwallador were a part might be considered to be the first Non-Jurors because they stood *mutatis mutandis* by the Protestation or Oath of Allegiance that they had made to Queen Elizabeth and rejected the Oath of 1606.

The entry for Father Robert Jones, SJ, in the *Dictionary of Welsh Biography*, credits him with stiffening the backbone of the English clergy in opposing the Oath of Allegiance. Doctor William Bishop, Robert Drurie and Roger Cadwallador made their stand on grounds of conscience and in obedience to papal diktat, and refused the Oath[5] without Fr Jones' intervention. But on the morning of his martyrdom, Blessed Roger was visited by two persons, one of whom is thought to have been Robert Jones, and was helped to make a 'good death'.

The pressure to swear to the Oath was to lead to the martyrdom of others beside Drurie and Cadwallador. These were Atkinson, Almond, Thulis, Arrowsmith, Herst, Gervase, Thomas Garnett, Gavan and Heath.

Notes

1   *Capture of Roger Cadwallador* (from Westminster Manuscripts, Vol. IX, 1610, in Belmont collection).
2   'The Oath of Allegiance', (http://faculty.history/.wisc.edu/sommerville), 2013.
3   'Robert Bellarmine', (Wikipedia).
4   'Tridentine Catholicism', (Wikipedia).
5   'English Post-Reformation Oaths', (Catholic Encyclopedia, online).

CHAPTER 15

'I stood in the listes'

ON THE MONDAY OF EASTER WEEK Blessed Roger was dragged from imprisonment, possibly in Hereford Castle, by the High Sheriff's men for an examination by the Bishop.[1] He would have been led under the timber-framed gatehouse of the Bishop's Palace which leads to the courtyard and from there into the twelfth-century Great Hall which today may be the oldest secular building in England. It is very imposing, being fifty-five feet wide and seventy- five feet long and much of its huge timber arcading remains today.

In the custody of seven or eight guards and his gaoler, Roger was manhandled into the presence of the Bishop. He wrote to a 'Reverend Friend' who had offered him support, and whom he trusted to continue to help, about what happened next:

> About two of the afternoon [I was] carried before ye Bishop and then left in the lower end of ye great chamber whilst ye Under Sheriff conferred in privat with the Bishop and showed him ye Church Stuffe which he had taken.

Any one of the articles referred to as 'Church Stuffe' would have been enough evidence to condemn the prisoner for the treason of being a papist priest. In the vast hall Roger witnessed the Bishop's glee from a distance of twenty metres. He describes what he saw:

> As I stood afare the under sherife shewed me unto ye Bishop who seeing me seemed exceeding joyfull that I was fallen into his hands as I did gather by his countenance. You are the man we

looke for, quoth the Bishop, why then, quoth he, you may call your neighbours and rejoice and be glad, alluding to that parable of the lost sheepe. And without delay I was called into an inner parlour.

The inner parlour appears to have been prepared for the examination. The priest writes that there was a table. In pictures of the time the table is often covered with a tapestry or woven rug. Those seated at the table are often shown wearing black and either a cap, if they were clerics, or tall stovepipe hats. Roger Cadwallador, standing on the other side of the table, was faced by an unfriendly committee and had armed guards behind him.

Roger knew that he had a great deal of prayerful support in the county. He had, somehow, already received a letter from a 'Reverend Sir' who had been contacted by Anthony (possibly Scrope), to help Blessed Roger with his defence. He describes his Reverend friend as: 'So live a member are you of that bodye whereof each one is careful and compassionate with the other'. It is helpful to us in our search that he was anxious to provide as much information as possible in his account and letters to assist 'that bodye' in his defence.

There were seated the Superintendent, as Roger calls the Bishop, the Chancellor, a Mr Hoskyns, and a Mr Richardson. Also present were one or two ministers who stood bareheaded with certain others who are not named. The Bishop's secretary was present with 'penn and Inke and Pap to take my examination'.

Guarding the prisoner were the Under-Sheriff, the gaoler and seven or eight men who would have stood behind and to the side of the prisoner. In a letter written later that week, Blessed Roger refers to this first examination as the time when 'I stood in the listes, poor wretch that I am to combate in the quarrel of Christe', standing opposite this carefully assembled group of his accusers, waiting for the questioning to start. Not surprisingly he was apprehensive. He describes himself at this point as 'Not yet free of fyghtes without nor fyghtes within'.

In a letter only three or four days later describing these examinations, he admits that he was afraid because he thought that he might be charged as a common criminal or a traitor:

> I was not a little troubled, for to you I will confess my faulte. When I understood what the enemy designed against me ... to attaine me with the crime of sedition. I was very loathe, as well as for myself as in this time when the priesthood is impugned, to be put to death as a malicious malefactor.

He had now entered the lists to 'combate in the quarel of Christe', which could only be done by 'living or dyinge' in the cause of the One with 'whose helpe' he writes, 'I nothinge doubt to winne the victory'. He would say whatever was necessary to make sure that he was condemned for his priesthood.

There began a series of questions which at first he did not answer. Then he said that this was not a fit examination as there was not a single accuser there to charge him with any crime. He said that they had no right to examine him without telling him what he was alleged to have done. He added that there was not a land in the whole world where a man was expected to accuse himself in the absence of any charge being brought against him.

The Bishop fell into his trap and urged him, upon his conscience, to confess whether he was a priest or not. As this was the question he hoped to elicit he acknowledged without more ado both his priesthood and his right name, saying that he was Roger Cadwallador. He added that he presumed that being a priest would not be considered a crime, especially in the presence of a bishop whose duty it was to maintain the dignity and honour of the priesthood.

> Why my Lord are not you, yourself, a priest? For I will make it appeare that if you be no priest you cannot possibly be a Bishop. For so much is well known to all ye learned that never was any man accounted as a lawfull Bishop who had not been first a priest.

He then asked for books to prove what he had said. The books were refused. Bishop Bennet was now on dangerous ground. His churchmanship was very different from that of traditional Anglicans such as the late queen and the Elizabethan Richard Hooker, who had retired to the country. Others, including the King, Lancelot Andrewes and Richard Bancroft, who had become Archbishop of Canterbury, would not have shared the Bishop's views nor would many of the traditionalist clergy in the Close. The Bishop declared that he was a priest, not a sacrificing priest, but one who was a 'spiritual' priest offering a sacrifice of thanksgiving. Not, he declared, a priest like Cadwallador 'that is called in Greek IDEOS and in Latin sacerdos'. He went further and utterly denied that Christ appointed any priests in the New Testament. Roger responded, 'Marrye, this is as much as I would desire, for now you have granted that you are no Bishop in ye Church of Christ saying that you are not truly and properly a priest'.

If the Bishop continued to insist on a low doctrine of the priesthood he was putting his episcopal status at risk and effectively denying that the King was a consecrated king. James I was known to have said, 'No bishop, no king'. By introducing Greek and Latin into the debate the bishop had effectively given the prisoner his head. A scholar to his fingertips and deeply immersed in studying the Fathers of the Church and with more than a working knowledge of Latin and Greek as well as Hebrew, Blessed Roger called on his knowledge of them to prove the orthodoxy of his beliefs. He spoke of the first Nicene Council, St Gregory Nazianzen, St John Chrysostom and St Augustine and the many books that the latter two had written about the priesthood. St Augustine, he said, mentions two kinds of priest, one spiritual such as all Christians are and the other sort that are truly and properly priests as the Church holds them to be.

Once again he asked for his books but they would not let him have them. Mr Hoskyns, who Roger later wrote had been sent to preserve the Bishop from embarrassment, had, it appears, been listening to the argument with some respect. He interjected that he thought that nothing could be proved out of St Augustine because the saint had never allowed any propitiatory sacrifice for the living and the dead.

Roger's response was that if he had St Augustine's book of *Confessions* then he would gladly show Mr Hoskyns where it was written that he allowed and recommended sacrifice for his mother's soul and that St Augustine had meant a sacrifice which takes away our sins. For a while Mr Hoskyns did not speak.

For the second time the prisoner was asked whether he was a priest or not and once again he freely confessed it and again gave his name. Then they asked him time and time again questions which would have had dangerous consequences for his parishioners about the dates and places that he had said Mass. He did not answer these questions.

It was said to have been a long examination and the Bishop was irritated by firstly being bettered in an argument in front of his ministers and secondly by having failed to illicit any information from him that would have helped him to get rid of any other Catholics in his diocese. He said that Christ was the only 'sacrifycinge' priest and therefore Roger Cadwallador could not claim to be one. Using every weapon in his intellectual armoury to focus the examination on the priesthood, Roger responded with a smile which the Bishop took for insolence, 'Make that good, I pray you, my lord, for so you will prove that I am no more a priest than other men, and consequently no more a traitor nor offender against your law'.

Mr Hoskyns intervened to try to calm the situation between the angry Bishop and the scholarly priest who was doing everything he could to provoke. He knew that the King, who was deeply committed to the new Oath of Allegiance, hoped to win the day with superior arguments. Clearly the Bishop of Hereford was failing in his attempt to persuade Roger Cadwallador to take the Oath. In addition he may have gained some respect for him during the exchanges which had led up to this moment. He is reported to have said to the Bishop,

I assure you, my lord, it is strange to see the alacrity and courage of those kind of men. I heard his Majesty with his own mouth say in the present parliament, that the number and courage of this kind of men is so great, that if I should, quoth he, put them to death as often as they fall into my hands, I believe I should never have done.

The Bishop would not listen to advice or let it go and said that there is no mention of priests in the New Testament. Once again his arguments were squashed by the prisoner. The word 'presbyter' was to be found in the New Testament, as were episcopos the stem of 'bishop' and *diaconos* from which came 'deacon'. Roger said, in the first Bible of Queen Elizabeth, at I Timothy, Chap. 4, v. 14, the word *presbyterii* is translated as 'priesthood'.

The Chancellor snapped at him angrily, wondering how he dared to think that he could justify his religion as well as the Bishop could his. It had been a long interrogation and the exhausted priest was outnumbered by at least twelve to one. Roger replied, 'I could better defend a good religion than he a badde'.

Given the character of the accused priest it is most likely that this was a considered reply. It was a response which could not be taken for equivocation which had brought such ridicule on the Jesuits at the time of the Gunpowder Treason. In addition, it may be that this response secured his condemnation for his Roman Catholic priesthood and the right to die as a martyr rather than as a 'malicious malefactor'. Roger Cadwallador was extraordinarily astute and later events show that he never yielded even under extreme pressure. It is hard to believe that his words were not carefully chosen.

His interrogators began to insult him. At the time, dress and appearance defined a man's status and there were certain fabrics and embellishments which it was against the law to wear unless one was of a certain 'quality'. The examination of the prisoner turned to insult and mockery. They scoffed at him for not shaving his head and his beard and for going about as a layman in his attire.

He wrote later that he was not dressed in any way that was exceptional, although his clothing was lighter in colour than theirs but his accusers implied that it was inappropriate. They made a lot of what he later described as a 'little silk point'. A point was a tagged piece of ribbon or cord used for tying hose at the knee.

They accused him of the grievous sin of swearing because he had said, 'in good faith' and 'of my truth'. In response, when writing the details of his examination to his Reverend Friend, he said that they must have very tender consciences indeed to describe his responses as swearing. At the time Roger Cadwallador, the gentleman's son and higher in social status than the Bishop, made no reply to their insults which exasperated and angered Bennet.

The King would have been pressing the Bishop to get the signature of this high profile Catholic priest on the King's Oath of Allegiance and now the Bishop urged it on him ferociously, but the prisoner resisted saying that he would not argue for or against but he would not take it.

The Bishop then committed Blessed Roger to prison. He gave the Gaoler strict instructions not to let him out of his sight. He thundered out threats against him if he allowed the prisoner to escape and emphasised that the man was to make sure that there were enough guards to make rescue impossible.

Note

1 *Examination 1&2, and imprisonment in Hereford and Leominster, of Roger Cadwallador* (from Westminster Manuscripts, Vol. IX, 1610 and quotations from his letters kept at Belmont).

CHAPTER 16

The Second Examination

A FTER THE FIRST EXAMINATION Blessed Roger had become unwell with a sweating sickness. The Keeper and his wife took care not to afford him any comfort but made every effort to bar him from any solace that the Catholic community might offer. When his brother's wife came to bring him a small bowl of nourishing broth, she was refused entry. She was reviled by the keeper's wife who said that she was her brother-in-law's concubine and that she would fling the broth into the street rather than let him have it. There was nothing but unkindness in their behaviour. They daily heaped fresh hurts on him and sometimes gave out that he had yielded and promised to recant if he could have a benefice. These insults of the keeper and his wife were unfounded and Blessed Roger is said to have patiently endured them but his situation was wretched.

Roger had a second examination by the Bishop shortly after the first one. When the Bishop called for him, as he was led out of the prison, he fainted. Later he wrote[1]:

> Brought before ye Bishop, when he saw how sicke and faynt I was he berated his man that would cause me in such plight to be brought thither. Yet being come (though I earnestlie intreated to be dismissed) he said that he would surlie bayte me for one whole hower.

Roger was to record that he thought Bishop Bennet was feigning concern and had no intention of letting his captive off the hook. He had brought into the Great Hall a cartload of books either in preparation for the examination or to insult the priest who had twice asked for books at his first examination. He had assembled four of his ministers who were closest to him. These clerics the priest named as the Chancellor and Dr Richardson, the Preacher. (After the Elizabethan Settlement, the country had seen the introduction of 13,000 preachers licensed to evangelise. The clergy who were not licensed had to read from a Book of Homilies when a preacher was not present.) Also among the four were Mr Vaughan and a Mr Kisley who is reported to have said very little. The Bishop and his henchmen baited Blessed Roger for the promised hour.

They asked him many questions especially about priesthood and marriage. Roger's response was that he held the Bishop's marriage to be as lawful as any other man's but said that if the Catholic Church had for centuries, and by her priests' own consent, forbidden marriage why should it concern them? The Bishop stated that St Paul was a married man. Blessed Roger replied that this was in flat contradiction to what St Paul said in 1 Corinthians, Chapter 7, v. 8: 'But I say to the unmarried, and to the widows: It is good for them if they continue, even as I'. Probably every single one of the assembled clerics would have known that it would have been better to cite St Peter when arguing for a married priesthood. St Peter's mother-in-law had been healed by Our Lord, which indicates that he was married. Perhaps it was that they were intimidated by the Bishop's intolerance of criticism to draw attention to his mistake. After an hour, Roger asked to be excused from more questions because of his pitiful weakness which had become so apparent that Bishop Bennet gave it up and dismissed his ministers. Then, once again, the Bishop roared out terrible threats against the gaoler if he allowed his prisoner to escape and he ordered him to take the priest back to his cell.

In the final section of a letter to his 'Reverend Friend', Roger expressed happiness and relief at the outcome of the examinations before the Bishop which had resulted in his being condemned for his priesthood alone. He was still hopeful that his Reverend Friend would be able to help him but he said:

I wish that whatever is most for the glory of God: be yt imprison-ment, banyshment or whatsoever. Specially if my imprisonment be ordinary as now it is not: for I have ben keepte in heavie irons (besides other inconveniences known to this place) night and daye, and now of late chained to the bedd post every nyght, but all this I can well endure. This comes out of the fear or hardnesse of the keeper, for otherwise I have the favour of the towne and countrye.

While he was in Hereford, his friends tried to visit him but were absolutely debarred from doing so and were unable to do him 'ye office which common courtesy requires'.

Bishop Robert Bennet had placed him in the hands of a gaoler who was terrified of his episcopal and political masters and would stop at nothing to placate them. He had first placed the priest in shackles and then, in response to the Bishop's threats, had added another set of shackles and a great 'bolt'. Eventually, because of Roger's sickness, the bolt was removed and occasionally one set of shackles, but they were replaced when the gaoler felt like it. In spite of all the hurts and insults heaped upon him, Blessed Roger reflected in a letter written soon after the two examinations:

Blessed be God, the enemy failed in his purpose. I am free from all misdemeanours and here remayne condemned and imprisoned only for my priesthood wherein I glory.

Note

1   Letters of Blessed Roger from the Belmont Archives.

CHAPTER 17

Leominster

BECAUSE OF AN OUTBREAK of plague in Hereford, the summer Assizes were held in Leominster.[1] Roger Cadwallador was transferred to the prison in the town:

> He was forced to go all the way on foot, feeble and weak as he was with bad usage and sickness together, yet he could not obtain to be free from his shackles in his journey, but it was thought a sufficient favour that a boy was permitted to go by his side, to bear up by a string the weight of some iron links which were wired to the shackles.

It was a strange procession that wended its way over Dinmore hill that day in the late spring of 1610. The boy would have gone ahead of the priest hauling the chains attached to the string. Slowly and painfully Roger limped along a pace or two behind the child trying to keep in step so as to prevent the drag of the shackles on his ankles. There was, apart from his Gaoler, in all likelihood a considerable number of guards. They were making an exhibition of him and perhaps hoped to provoke a rescue which would have given them an excuse to kill him. Friends of the accused may have been hiding in the shadows, feeling helpless but knowing that their priest had accepted whatever outcome God had in mind for him, yet hoping to hearten him. They also gave the Gaoler an audience.

All the way to Leominster Blessed Roger is said to have been in great pain but endured it all patiently while throughout the journey his Gaoler is said to have reproached him, calling him 'Traytor and many other evil charges' and said that he, 'himself was a better man than this reverend priest'. It would appear that the Gaoler had been well schooled in saying what was most provoking and insulting. Past records show that the Leominster Gaoler had been the Town Crier and, if this was still the case, as well as bawling out his insults the gaoler may have preceded that grotesque parody of a procession with the ringing of a bell. He would have been dressed for the occasion in his official 'blew fries coote and crimson kersey hose', meaning his Town Crier uniform of a blue coat and bright red stockings.

When the priest arrived in Leominster he was taken to the local gaol at the end of Church Street near to the Priory church. There had been a prison in Leominster for centuries. It was located just inside what was known in medieval days as the inner Gate of the town, which was also the West Gate of the Priory Church. The prison stood on the south side of the road. It was a strong two-storey building with the Gaoler's lodge close by. The Borough Records show that Leominster Gaol was well equipped with bolts and irons, manacles and cords as well as a whipping post.

Once again Roger was in the hands of an unusually cruel man in the shape of Kyngman, the Leominster Gaoler and, as in Hereford, he was kept in chains. His health was giving his family and friends cause for concern but now at least, although in strictly controlled circumstances, he was occasionally allowed visitors.

Roger was often sick when he was in prison and he was subject to ill-usage and slanders. Throughout those dark days he maintained his cheerfulness and courage according to the records of his friends. Once when he was prostrated by sickness he lay shaking his shackles and is reported to have said to a notable visitor: 'The High Priest of the old law had little bells about the rim of his vestements, and I stirring my legs say, Audi, Domine, haec sunt tintinnabula mea [Hear, O Lord! These are my little bells]'. In this way he signified that the sound of his shackles was as acceptable to God as the sound of the High Priest's little bells. He was referring to Ecclesiasticus, Chapter 45, vv. 6–12, which is about Aaron who had been given the high priesthood among the people. It contains the verse: 'He clothed him with a robe of glory, and compassed him with many little bells of gold, that a noise might be heard in the temple for a memorial to the children of his people'.

There are a number of homely stories supplied by local people and the family of Blessed Roger at the time which illustrate what his imprisonment in Leominster must have been like. On one occasion his Gaoler tried to trick Blessed Roger into betraying himself. He admitted a boy with learning difficulties who is described as a 'sillye' youth of twenty-two years of age who was not a Catholic, to speak to the priest and to offer to do some errands for him. After he had done so the Gaoler enticed the youth into a private chamber and stripped and searched him, perhaps to find details of a plot, but found nothing. He then sent the boy into the town to carry out the tasks the priest had asked him to do. When he returned the youth was stripped naked again presumably to check to make sure that he had not been given anything that might incriminate Roger by a friend of his on the outside. After this humiliating exercise they released the boy. When he had departed a little way out of the town the Gaoler and some others pursued him saying, 'hold ye traytor'. Two strong men outran the others and took hold of the simple youth and brought him back. A large crowd had assembled and watched, with a mounting sense of outrage, as, in the porch of the Priory, they removed all the young man's clothes but, of course, again found nothing. His captors were enjoying themselves too much to let him go and the Gaoler continued his torment by taking the boy into his prison and locking him in a chamber for a whole day and night.

A worthy gentleman of Leominster who suspected that the boy had done nothing wrong went to the bailiff to ask him who was in charge in the town, 'the bailiff or Kyngman the gaoler?' The bailiff went to remonstrate with the Gaoler and told him that he had far exceeded his authority and asked him for an explanation. The Keeper's response is not recorded. The Gaoler appears to have been an exceptionally cruel and unpleasant man who terrorised his wife, but she, in spite of her fear of him, had engineered the boy's escape by a back door. The friendship of the priest and the Gaoler's wife is touching and must have been a blessing for them both as they were the victims of a gratuitously cruel man. This account may have come from her. It might be that we owe a debt of gratitude to the Gaoler's wife for the safe delivery of his letters to his friends. She was in daily contact with him and someone must have hidden and carried them for him although fear of her husband, especially after the sentencing, would have limited this activity.

John Cadwallador was only once allowed to visit his brother in the Forbury gaol. On that occasion the Gaoler detained him and would not let him go until he had handed over five shillings, a large amount in those days.

Note

1   Belmont papers.

CHAPTER 18

'We shall meet again'

ROGER CADWALLADOR'S FAMILY and friends appear to have been growing increasingly anxious. It was as difficult then as it is now to watch the suffering of a loved one, especially if one feels that it could be prevented. The sufferer can appear to be stubborn and selfish, and their steadfastness and ultimate altruism not appreciated. The witty and erudite Dean of St Paul's, John Donne,[1] had grown up in a recusant household and, through his parents, was related to Thomas More and more than one Catholic martyr. In his eyes his family had suffered 'in their persons and fortunes for obeying the Teachers of Romane Doctrine'. State propaganda at the time of Blessed Roger said that those who assented to the Oath of Allegiance to King James I were 'harassed by a papal decree, which came in with Birket, whereby they were deprived of all their jurisdiction and consigned to penury and ignominy'. It may be that his family and friends who loved him may have shared some of the same feelings about Church doctrine as John Donne when they heard of his distress.

In making a stand, the martyr is a hero to some and a villain to others and it is always a lonely position.[2] Blessed Roger's letters do not suggest that he had been brought to such a wretched position for the reasons of doctrine or dogma but for a deep love of God expressed through his priesthood. His own response to his family and friends is the best defence of his position[3]:

> You write to her some comforte from me. I pray you let this be your comforte, that I am merry and well in the way to the endlesse

comforte, which the Holy Ghost the Comforter make me to enjoye. In this you shoulde take comforte, rather than in my present life and libertie, except you seeke your own comfort and not myne.

In a letter before his first examination by the Bishop of Hereford he had described himself subject to 'fyghtes without and fyghtes within'. It would appear that these very human feelings never left him.

He did not seek martyrdom but he accepted it. Patiently he goes on to remind them of an incident in his childhood,

Remember I pray you my humble dutie to my mother. She can tell, for I have often heard my father speake of yt, that when I was in my childhood dangerously sicke, he made a vow or prmse to God that if I recovered, he would bestow me on him, therefor I pray you be not offended yf our Lord take this same right due to him by so many titles. I will say no more but be merry in God and never be sory that my soule is in the road of safety.

Fare you well.

This is all the reassurance he can give them because, as he goes on to write, 'comfortable news of my libertie you longe to he[a]r of that I know nothing nor have not heard any word of such matter this longe time'.

The cost to Blessed Roger of accepting what God asked of him is clear in the statements he writes which indicate his loneliness and distress. He refers briefly to old friends, his 'trustid John of Hereford' and his 'best beloved Anthony' expressing sorrow that they had not made contact and asked that they do what they could to sue for his liberty as he did not have the means to do so. He must have known how difficult it was for those closest to him to make contact but in spite of his being able to understand their problems his situation was wretched and his isolation would have been very difficult to bear. He seems to have understood their uncertainties and tried to reassure his family and friends that there was still hope. At the end of a letter he wrote:

> God's blessing on you and yours. I am not yet worthy to be a martyr and seeing your comforte is in my life, you need not be discomforted for ought I know.

This was to change as he was soon to know his fate. It may have been in June or July at the Summer Assizes of 1610, in Leominster, that he was condemned as a priest, it is thought for 'taking orders beyond the sea'. The sentence of death was probably given in the small chapel of St Thomas of Canterbury now called the Forbury chapel. A description of what was to happen at his execution would have been read out to him. He would not have been spared a single, gruesome detail.

He wrote to his friends knowing that now without doubt 'he was near to his crown':

> Comfort yourselves, my friends, in this, that I die in assurance of salvation; which if you truly love me, as you ought to do, should please you better, than to have me alive a little while among you for your content, and then to die with great uncertainty, either to be saved or damned. If the manner of my death be shameful, yet no more than my Saviour's was; if it be painful, yet no more than my Saviour's was. Only take care to persevere in God's true faith and charity and then we shall meet again to our greater comfort that shall never end.
>
> Fare ye well.

Notes

1   A.N. Wilson, *The Elizabethans* (London: Hutchinson, 2011), p. 202.
2   L.B. Smith, *Fools, Martyrs, Traitors* (New York: Alfred A. Knopf, 1997), pp. 3–20.
3   Quotations taken from Roger Cadwallador's letters, kept at Belmont.

CHAPTER 19

Last Days

AFTER HIS SENTENCE OF EXECUTION, Roger Cadwallador could have had no doubt that he was on a journey that, in a short time, would take him to his death. His condemnation for the crime of being a priest ordained abroad appeared to have caused Kyngman the Gaoler to increase his efforts to goad him into recanting by more and more vicious punishments.

The account says that, three days after he was sentenced to die, his Keeper chained him every night to the bed with a great chain. Occasionally, early in the morning, he would take the priest into a 'vile room' and chain him to a post. He could walk no further than the length of the chain, which was two yards at the most, and this was as much scope as he had for exercise. There was nowhere for him to sit down or relieve himself. On one occasion he remained there for five or six hours until the Gaoler's wife released him, taking advantage of the fact that her husband was out of town at that time.

There is a later description of this 'vile room' in a report relating to Leominster Quakers[1] who were taken out of Meetings for refusing to swear the Oath of Allegiance and chained up,

> in a little close nasty Hole, where they were forced to lie on Straw, and sometimes so crowded that they had not Room to lie down all at once. Besides they were constrained to ease their Bodies in the same Place which for want of cleansing was become so loathsome, that those who came to speak to them through the Hole of the Door could hardly endure the Stench for a few Minutes.

The Gaoler's Turnkey, sent to release a woman prisoner, was heard to say, 'It was not fit to put a Dog in'.

Roger was not allowed visitors, with one or two very rare exceptions, and so was deprived of the opportunity to make his last wishes known. Wills were important in the settling of affairs before death in the presence of family, friends and neighbours. This was another deprivation that he and those he loved would have felt deeply.

Except through Blessed Roger's letters and those of others, it is not possible to know what the priest was thinking and feeling, especially as he was protective of his friends and conscious of the need to keep them out of harm's way.

Following the Martyr's death, the Jesuit Vice-Prefect, Fr Robert Jones, sent a letter, in Italian, to the Cardinal-Protector Bellarmine, which was his personal account of what happened to Roger, before and during his execution. This letter records a visit to the priest whom he had contrived to see on his last day on earth. This letter, while it is illustrative of Roger's importance in the Catholic world, was not accepted in Herefordshire as a fair report of the circumstances surrounding the death of the martyr because it disparaged the efforts of his neighbouring brethren while he was in prison.

A letter in the Belmont archives, dated 28 October 1610, from John Jennings, described as the Franciscan, and a Secular priest who is not named, was written to refute the version of events in Father Jones' Italian letter. The Franciscan and the Secular priest had been subjected to an enquiry following Fr Jones' report to his Superior in Rome, and wrote the following to defend themselves. The Secular says:

> They were strangers to this shyer or misinformed that so reported of us, for non knew his estate better than I nor whom he used more familierly being neare neyboures. Often he hath Complained to me of ther unkindness though it was one of ther good happes to doe that great acte of Charitie upon him which we were all glad of for we knew that ther had bene heretofore much unkindness between them and him.

In their letter, the Franciscan and the Secular respond to what must have seemed a hurtful calumny by Robert Jones. They certify each other against the Jesuit's charge that Roger Cadwallador had little respect or comfort from his secular 'brethren'. Their complaint about the Italian letter is that it suggests that the only 'favour and charity' Blessed Roger received 'were shewed him by this Companye', meaning 'The Jesuits'. They had in their possession 'swete' letters from Blessed Roger which would refute this version of events and which they had shown to a Mr Martin, who was acting for the unknown person of importance to whom their letter is addressed. To the charges of neglect made against them they responded:

> Neyther Mr Jennings nor I ever fayled him but shewed him all humanitie we could by sending him money and books from tyme to tyme and comforting him by letters and offering furder to have visited him but he refused it wishing non to adventure themselves to such danger but desired our prayers only as by his letters to us both he testifyed.

Made anxious by the accusations in the Italian letter, they write that if what they had certified is not enough:

> If it doe not suffice I knowe all my brethren adjoining will testify as much but we could not mete together conveniently by reason of waters and dangers of the tyme etc.

The confusion caused by the lack of a will is described as a bear without a leader. Fr Jones claimed that the martyr had made him a bequest of his books on the morning of his death but this is questioned:

> Furder they reported in that Italian letter that he bequeathed them his library whereupon I examined his brother and another gentleman a very honest man . . . severally. And they both constantly affirme that he sould his library – at his first apprehension.

There is no doubt from the record that he was very grateful for the kindness shown to him by the Jesuits on the day of his death.

Recently there has been some research into the Jesuit books from the Cwm in Herefordshire, then the Jesuit College of St Francis Xavier, which are now cared for in the Hereford Cathedral archives. Nothing has yet been traced to Roger Cadwallador.

There was another problem relating to the estate which concerns the Franciscan and the Secular, and they ask for help because they have received only ten pounds which is very little as they say 'amongst soe many poore Catholics as be heare in his own Countrey'. They are sure that his will has been perverted and his gift bestowed they know not how. They ask for the investigator's help to recover it or at least to inform them where it has gone.

The end of the letter is very formal and it would appear that the Franciscan and the Secular had been the subject of an important enquiry into their conduct as a result of the Italian letter. The anxiety engendered by the letter illustrates the huge significance of Roger Cadwallador's martyrdom at that time. The end of the letter is very respectful: 'This with our humble dewty remembered; submitting ourselves to your sentence and censure. Yours ever to command Jo. Jenninges.'

There is another letter which may yield some very limited clues as to what happened to Blessed Roger's estate. The names included in a letter written in Latin are in code but the tone of the letter is one of gratitude. It was, as the Franciscan and the Secular would have said, a 'swete' letter. It was addressed to an unnamed priest who is said to be carefully guarding the things that Roger left behind and thanks an anonymous woman who has been working hard and devotedly on his account for the great good of others.

Roger knew that it was not possible to take anything with him on his journey home to God. He may already have been aware of how his estate had been distributed. Not wishing to cling to goods and relationships of this present world appears to have given him a very pragmatic view of his own death. From prison he wrote to friends asking that a collection should be made after his death and that it should be disposed of for the good of others as the contributors thought proper. He suggested that a solicitor who was described as a very honest man of his profession and employed in most 'Catholick concerns' should be consulted and recorded his name as 'Mr Fisher, Next door to Mr Sherwood, Surgeon, In Devonshire Street near Red Lyon Square, London'. The names of other priests including George Nappier, who died for his religion, are recorded as clients of Mr Fisher. The most precious bequest that Blessed Roger made was to a Secular priest, John Stephens, a neighbouring missionary. He wrote to him giving him the care of his flock. In his last days and without the support of those he loved he had done his best to dispose of his earthly goods. All that was left now was to complete his earthly journey.

The person who shared his last hours was a lay Catholic prisoner, Mr Powel. There is nothing in the record to tell us any more than that he was there at the last and went to the scaffold with Blessed Roger.

The Gaoler had not finished with the priest and the Belmont account records that 'Some howers before his execution, his keeper of set purpose took occasion to move him to impatience as much as his mischievous mind could'. The record continues 'but God be thanked he was no whit at all distempered'.

Note

1   N.C. Reeves, *The Town in the Marches* (Leominster: Orphans Press, 1972), pp. 96–97.

CHAPTER 20

'The long desired day'

'*THE LONG DESIRED DAY WHEREIN he was to suffer*' came at last. Roger Cadwallador and Mr Powel left their beds at three o'clock on the morning of 27 August 1610, the day of their execution, and were on their knees in prayer until eight o'clock.[1] As the sun rose, crowds of people were drawn to the Forbury gaol in the hope of seeing the priestly prisoner. They came from the country as well as the town and were to continue to gather for the rest of the day. Many of these people were strangers to him but all who came gave evident signs of their compassion and their wish to offer their support in those last hours. Through streaming tears they protested that they would undertake to walk barefoot for hundreds of miles if it would do him any good. Roger accepted their goodwill with gratitude. He thanked them courteously. Gently he reassured them that he considered it a glorious thing to die for Christ and the Catholic Faith.

The last day of Blessed Roger is recorded in great detail and so we know that at about ten o'clock he took 'a little comfortable broth'. After this the Gaoler brought two visitors in to see him. One of these men is thought to have been the Jesuit, Father Robert Jones. It was a very clever and Jesuitical contrivance to have gained entry at such a time and may have employed equivocation. It is not clear how they persuaded Kyngman to let them in to see the prisoner unless they told him that they were going to raise the question of the Oath. This was the truth, as they did raise it, but not in the way that the gaoler would have wished. However it was managed, the Jesuit did Roger Cadwallador the great service of hearing his confession and is said to have shown him a great deal of compassion.

Apparently heartened by his good confession and the support of brother priests, Blessed Roger began to talk to his visitors about the King's Oath of Allegiance and compared himself to Bishop John Fisher of Rochester who had accepted his need for physical as well as spiritual strengthening. Using the Bishop as an example, he called for a pint of claret sweetened with sugar and toasted his friend, declaring, as St John Fisher had said, when he took it 'for his better undertaking so greate a combate as ye combate of death which he shortlie after overcame'. Sustained by the wine, he repeated Bishop Fisher's quotation from the psalms 'fortitudinem meam ad te custodiam'. He is said to have 'Englished' it into 'I will keep my strength for the Lord'.

Then Blessed Roger said something which may have indicated a moment of uncertainty: 'The Bishop suffered Martirdome onlie for refusing an othe'. His visitors appear to have been prepared for a moment of hesitation and the one who had come in with the Jesuit told him that 'Mr Drurie suffered likewise for the like refusal and that he himself was an eye-witness of his glorious martyrdome'. Robert Drurie's courageous death meant that he was no longer alone in making his stand. He was a Secular priest and co-signatory to the Appeal for a Bishop. He had also signed the Protestation of Allegiance of 1603 but refused the King's Oath of 1606. For this he had been hung drawn and quartered at Tyburn in 1607. The account continues, 'this reverend priest Mr Cadwallador seemed much to rejoice and said that as Mr Drurie and I was true loving friends heer on earth soe he did not doubt but they should be yoke-fellowes in heaven'.

The visitors then did him one last service and provided him with new clothing to replace, from head to foot, the sorry rags that he had been wearing in prison. Roger appears to have been delighted by the fresh smell and feel of new clothes as he put on his 'wedding garments'. Then he took his leave of his friends with many good and Godly exhortations to persevere in the Catholic Faith. As they left he asked them to give his fellow prisoner, Mr Powel, who must have been waiting separately, as much money as they could spare, which was said to have been twelve pence, for the Keeper. He kept back in the pocket of his hose two shillings for the person leading the horses which would draw the hurdle carrying him to the scaffold.

Spiritually, physically and emotionally prepared, he settled down to wait for the Under-Sheriff, Prychard, to arrive. Prychard was the same official who had arrested him on Easter Day and was now to accompany him to 'that bloody designments' which awaited him at the crossroads in Leominster.

Half an hour before he was to suffer, Kyngman, the Keeper, 'for a farewell', used all his art and cunning to goad him and 'make him distempered with passion' but found him 'so well fenced with patience' that it was all in vain and, giving it up, he went to fetch the Under-Sheriff.

Note

1   Account of last day taken from the Belmont Archives.

CHAPTER 21

'If the manner of my death be shameful, yet no more than my Saviour's was . . .'*

AT ABOUT FOUR O'CLOCK in the afternoon, the Under-Sheriff, James Prychard, arrived at the Forbury prison. He was accompanied by guards, Richard Kyngman the Gaoler, a man leading a horse drawing a hurdle and two masons who were to be the prisoners' executioners. The masons had on long black garments and wore black visors over their faces. The record says that their clothing made them appear 'ugly and dreadful'.

Emerging blinking into the sunlight after so many days' incarceration, Roger Cadwallador, 'the champion of Christ', appears to have been undaunted at the sight and is said to have cheerfully enquired, 'What is to be done?'

The Under-Sheriff replied, 'Nothing, sir, if you please; for if you will but take the Oath of Allegiance here, you may save us labour and yourself much pain.' The prisoner said that he was not prepared to take the oath. Prychard then asked him more than once to reconsider. The prisoner persisted in his refusal saying that he stood by his former resolution. Prychard said that in that case there was no help for him and he must lie down upon the hurdle.

The hurdle was the first of the penalties meted out at the prisoner's trial. He was to be drawn to his death backwards on a hurdle at a horse's tail. Because of his unnatural behaviour, his head

---

* All details cited in this chapter are taken from the Westminster Manuscripts, Vol. IX, 1610, kept in the Belmont Archives.

would be near the ground so that he would no longer be allowed to share the common air. Unwilling to concur in his own death, the priest put himself at the disposal of his executioners. Submitting himself to the black-clad masons he allowed them to take him by the arms and place him on the wicker hurdle and fasten him there with leather cords. He made the sign of the cross, as well as he could, and then it is written that he 'quietly betook himself to some heavenly contemplation. Like a patient and milde lambe now readie to be drawn to ye shambles'.

In a town, the place where the butchery was carried out was called the Shambles. Blessed Roger had paid the man who led the horse which drew the hurdle two shillings, not to make the journey easier for himself but as an act of forgiveness and recognition that in the end the man was doing him a service.

There is an old pavement on the left along the lane which leads to the church in Bodenham in Herefordshire which has been preserved and shows how very uneven the road surfaces would have been in those times. It would have been impossible to escape buffeting and bruising as he was dragged along his own personal Via Dolorosa.

The company left behind the Forbury prison and passed under the old Priory Gateway and along what was then St Andrew's street, with the horse's hooves clattering on the cobbles under the overhanging, many-gabled, timber houses of the old High Street to the Five Ways where there was once an iron cross. Traditionally this is the site of the martyrdom of Blessed Roger. It is known that at that time a raised platform was built for executions on which there were seats which could be purchased by those who were rich enough to pay for them and wanted the best view of the spectacle. Others, who on this occasion were a mixture of spectators and supporters of the prisoner, crowded round the dais. Behind them the hurdle was drawn to a halt.

Bruised and buffeted for a quarter of an hour, Blessed Roger lay on the hurdle apparently meditating on what was to come. It is written that he was asking for the strength to combat what lay ahead of him and the grace to achieve a Godly and happy end. Impatient with the delay, the Under-Sheriff stepped onto the hurdle with the Statute book in his hands. He promised the priest that if he would take the Oath of Allegiance he had the power to pardon him until the King's pleasure was known. Calmly Roger replied that he had made his resolution clear. 'No?' queried the Under-Sheriff, 'then the Lord have mercy on your soul.'

After that the prisoner's cords were loosed and he was lifted to his feet and taken to within sight of the gallows. They showed him the block on which he was to be quartered and 'those other great instruments of death', leading him between two great fires on which there were cauldrons of burning pitch, one to burn his heart and bowels, the other to boil his head and quarters. They thought that they would terrify him and promised that he would be untouched if he would but 'TAKE THE OATH'. Roger Cadwallador appeared to be unimpressed by these macabre toys and again refused to be tempted but 'like a constant captayne rested in his former resolution'.

When they led him to the ladder by which he was to ascend to the gallows, he knelt in prayer, apparently for some time. Some of the crowd were beginning to be restless and wanted the executioners to make an end and so claimed that night was beginning to fall. Perhaps the sky had darkened because at that time of the year, August, the night comes later.

Possibly feeling that they were losing any advantage they had, a second group sprang to their feet from amongst the front row of spectators and entered the 'quarrel'. They were Mr Thomas Coningsby, Mr Humfrey Cornwall and an old adversary from his examinations before the Bishop, Dr Richardson, the Preacher. These three with many 'fayr' promises tried to persuade him to take the Oath. They said that he would be doing God and his country a good service and that it would persuade others to follow his example. Blessed Roger remained 'an invincible champion and would not yield any consent'.

It was at this point that Roger felt it was time to speak. Turning to the crowd he protested his patriotism, acknowledging 'his Majesty to be true and lawful king of England, Scotland and Ireland'. He told them that he:

> was willing to swear his true allegiance as far as his conscience would allow which was as far as the laws of God and conscience might command all Subjects to be true to their Princes.

Evidently pleased with this response Mr Coningsby, Mr Cornwall and Dr Richardson, with some others present, asked him to proceed to the Oath as he had 'begune well'.

'There is some secret poison in the sequel', responded the priest. The learned gentlemen protested that there was nothing in the Act touching the Pope's authority and all it sought was allegiance to the King. Dr Richardson became very heated and importuned him for his refusal.

Roger then said that his own opinion counted for nothing. He said that his taking the Oath would neither diminish the Pope's real authority nor increase the King's. He was not prepared to discuss the matter any further. He was a man under authority and would defer to: 'Ye judgement of ye learned and ye censure of ye Catholique Church'.

After that he was taken to the ladder which he climbed a little way so that he could be seen by the people as he addressed them. He told them 'that he was to die for that he was a priest and come into his country to communicate ye Sacraments unto God's children and to draw those which resisted into the way of salvation'.

Blessed Roger's anxiety from the beginning of his trials had been that he would be condemned as a 'malicious malefactor' at a time when the priesthood was being impugned. He quoted the First Letter of St Peter which stresses the importance of dying for Christ and not to let the Faith be defamed by false and unacceptable imputations, as it says in Chapter IV, v. 15, 'but let none of you suffer as a murderer, or a thief, or a railer, or a coveter of other men's things'.

He was interrupted by Richardson who said that Cadwallador 'misapplied the place of Scripture, being to suffer for treason in the highest degree'. Mildly the priest replied:

> You mistake sir, I was condemned only for being a priest; and it is clear from the public proffers which have been made me, if I would condescend to take the new oath, that I am not guilty of treason in the highest degree.

His speech ended by his desiring all the people to 'Beare witness that he died a Catholique priest for ye Catholique cause' and then he entreated any Catholics present in the multitude that they would say a 'Pater Noster' and an 'Ave' with him, privately if they did not want to be identified as Catholics. Mr Coningsby said that he hoped that there were no such people present. When the prayers were finished Dr Richardson asked if he would say a 'Pater' with him. Roger smiled at his words and said that he would, 'if you will say one with me first'. The Preacher declined.

One of the executioners put the halter around his neck which he seemed to accept very patiently as the yoke of his Master. Then he freely forgave his executioners and all the others who were accessories to his death. He named Bishop Robert Bennet, who the account says had his fingers deepest in his blood, and said that he wished him a higher place in heaven than himself. He wished that he would be the last priest to die in England for the Catholic Faith.

His final deeply moving statement was the gift of his martyrdom for the sins of all dishonourable priests:

> That his blood might serve by the grace and merits of Christ to blot out and wipe out of memory whatever stain or blemish was to come to his country by the loose and scandalous lives of those that went in the name of Catholic priests.

He prayed privately for a few moments while the executioners came to turn the ladder and then he said aloud five or six times in

Latin, 'Into thy hands, O Lord, I commend my spirit' and then finally 'Lord receive my spirit'. Then the hangmen bundled Blessed Roger up to the top of the ladder and, with a push, sent him on his journey into the next world.

CHAPTER 22

'If it be painful, yet no more than my Saviour's was'

WHAT FOLLOWS IS AN EXTRACT FROM Richard Challoner's *Memoirs of the English Martyrs and Confessors,*[*] and is an eye-witness account:

He hung very long, and in extraordinary pain, by reason that the knot, through the unskillfulness of the hangman, came to be directly under his chin, serving only to pain, and not to despatch him. Insomuch, that when the people were persuaded that he was thoroughly dead, he put up his hand to the halter, as if he had either meant to show how his case stood, or else to ease himself; but bethinking himself better, and perhaps a scruple coming into his head to concur to hasten his own death; he had scarce touched the halter, but that he presently pulled away his hand. And within the space of a *Pater-Noster* after, he lifted up his hand again to make the sign of the cross; which made all the standers by, much amazed; and some of the vulgar, desirous to rid him of his pain, lifted him upwards by the legs twice or thrice, letting him fall again, with a swag. Then after a little rest, when they thought him quite dead, he was cut down; but when he was brought to the block to be quartered, before the bloody butcher could pull off his doublet, he revived and began to breathe; which the multitude perceiving, began to murmur; which made the under-sheriff cry out to the

---

[*] R. Challoner, *Memoirs of Missionary Priests and Other Catholics of Both Sexes That have Suffered Death in England on Religions Accounts from the Year 1577–1684* (Philadelphia: John T. Green, 1839), pp. 26–27.

executioner to hasten: but before they had stripped him naked, he was come to a very perfect breathing. It was long after they had opened him before they could find his heart, which notwithstanding, panted in their hands when it was pulled out. As soon as the head was cut off, one of the sheriff's men lifted it up on the point of his halbert, expecting the applause of the people, who made no sign that the fact was pleasing to them. Nay, they that were present were struck at the sight, and said, 'This priest's behaviour and death would give great confirmation to all the papists of Herefordshire': which saying fell out to be true: for it ministered them great courage and comfort.

So far my old manuscript.

CHAPTER 23

Martyrs

MARTYRS, WE ARE TAUGHT, bear witness to the heart of Christ's sacrifice: Roger Cadwallador surrendered his life into God's hands to do with as He saw fit. All martyrs make this sacrifice freely knowing that the present cost of their offering counts as nothing in comparison with life with the Lord who will receive them.

> But the souls of the virtuous are in the hands of God,
> No torment shall ever touch them.
> In the eyes of the unwise, they did appear to die;
> Their going like a disaster,
> Their leaving us, like annihilation;
> But they are in peace.
> If they experienced punishment as men see it,
> Their hope was rich with immortality;
> Slight was their affliction, great will their blessings be.
> God has put them to the test
> And proved them worthy to be with him;
> He has tested them like gold in a furnace,
> And accepted them as a holocaust. (Wisdom 3:1–6)

END PAPERS

MR CONINGSBY, who was present at the brutal proceedings, is said to have left early, apparently sickened at the horror of Blessed Roger's execution.

The archives contain a note which says that the two 'buchyards', Blessed Roger's executioners, could not get any work afterwards. The martyr's head is said to have been set up at the Cross House and his four quarters at different points in the town, namely Bargates, Lugg Bridge in Bridge Street, Battle Bridge in South Street and in Etnam Street. Also in the archives, another note says that in the place of one of his quarters a Leominster woman said that she saw a great light and, noisily, told everyone in the town.

In reference to the tragic events, the Borough Chamberlin's Accounts have an entry for 1610 which records an amount of money but the substance of the note which would have explained the costs is missing. Presumably it had been withdrawn because it was the cost of building the gallows and paying the Martyr's executioners, and was a source of shame.[1]

Gainsford Black, the Leominster historian, also writes,

> A careful search among the Archives of the Corporation has failed to find the 'note' referred to, which it is to be feared has been detached and mislaid, lost, or removed. It is somewhat singular that the Churchwardens' Accounts, are also missing for this year.[2]

No one has yet discovered where the Martyr's remains are buried. My personal view is that they may be buried in the old churchyard at Stretton. Roger Cadwallador's father had made provision for his own decent Christian burial, putting the overseeing of this in the hands of his wife Margaret and his younger son John, as well as the dear friend of both Rogers, William Morgan. A part of his will which was proved in 1610 is recorded in the first chapter. I believe that the people who loved him would have looked after the remains of Blessed Roger and placed them in the plot which had been purchased for his father and his forefathers with the same discretion and devotion which they had shown him throughout his life.

He is unique, according to Godfrey Anstruther, OP, in his book on Seminary Priests, in being the only martyr amongst those listed to have appeared after his death. This was to a wavering Catholic prisoner in Hereford.[3]

It is a very personal opinion, but I have been aware of his presence on more than one occasion when I have felt ready to give up. I know that at these times he was looking after me.

There is a relic of Roger Cadwallador in the Stonyhurst Museum. It is a diamond shaped piece of bone. It is thin and measures about 3cms by 1.5cms. It is thought to be part of a shin bone. The martyr's name is written on a slip of paper in a seventeenth-century hand, which is the same as on the slips attached to the other relics of English martyrs in the same frame. It is thought to have come from the Jesuit College of St Omer in 1592 which transferred to Bruges in 1762; from Bruges it probably went to Liege when the college moved there in 1773 and finally from Liege to Stonyhurst in 1794.

On 22 November 1987, Pope John Paul II announced the beatification of Roger Cadwallador. He was beatified among 1,340 other men and women. The Pope's action has been described as surprising everybody, and even embarrassing, as it might be seen as triumphalist and upset the sensitivities of those of other religions or denominations. It is important not to be drawn into this debate. The Pope did not resurrect Blessed Roger amongst a host of other holy men and women as, in medieval terms, a 'stinking Lazarus', that is one who, after being given the last rites, gets up from his death bed only to be shunned by the rest of the community. Nor did any of the 1,340 die in order to gain our recognition or approbation. John Paul II beatified a new model army of martyrs and confessors who, by their lives and deaths, refresh the seedbed of the Church.

In the words of Roger Cadwallador,

'Fare ye well'.

Notes

1 F. Gainsford Blacklock, *The Suppressed Benedictine Minster and Other Ancient & Modern Institutions of the Borough of Leominster* (Leominster: Centre Print Digital, 1999), p. 271.
2 *Ibid.*
3 Godfrey Anstruther, OP, *The Seminary Priests, Vol. 1, Elizabethan 1558–1603* (Gateshead: Northumberland Press Ltd, 1968), pp. 61–62. Reference to this appearance can be found in the Westminster Diocesan Archives, AAW XI, no. 25.
4 J.J. Norwich, *The Popes* (London: Vintage, 2012), pp. 448–449.

Lightning Source UK Ltd.
Milton Keynes UK
UKOW04f0738100815

256676UK00002B/84/P